GREAT FACES OF DORSET

# GREAT FACES
## *of* DORSET

*Photographs* MILLIE PILKINGTON
*Text* ELIZABETH POPE

THE DOVECOTE PRESS

First published in 2014 by The Dovecote Press Ltd
Stanbridge, Wimborne Minster, Dorset BH21 4JD

ISBN 978-0-9929151-0-0

Photographs © Millie Pilkington 2014
Text © Elizabeth Pope 2014

Typeset in Sabon and designed by The Dovecote Press Ltd
Printed and bound in India by Replika Press Pvt. Ltd.

All papers used by The Dovecote Press are natural, recyclable products
made from wood grown in sustainable, well-managed forests.

A CIP catalogue record for this book is available from the British Library

1 3 5 7 9 8 6 4 2

# Contents

# Introduction and Acknowledgements

The idea for *Great Faces of Dorset* first came to Millie at a chicken auction conducted by Richard Hicks, who sadly lives in Somerset so was not eligible for inclusion in the book. He had her enthralled with his auctioneer's banter, burgeoning facial hair and pork pie hat. She had the idea that she should document these very special characters with their curious occupations. In London it appears that many people's lives follow the same pattern but not so in the country. I was lucky enough to be given the chance to write the text to accompany her striking photographs, and so we began a three year journey of interviews and photo shoots, with many adventures and laughs along the way.

As our journey progressed we were struck by the warm welcomes we received in strangers' homes, the genuine interest and enthusiasm we were shown for the project and people's willingness to share, over a cup of tea, the stories of their fascinating lives. Some of the more elderly had us captivated and yearning for a life in rural Dorset as it was many years ago.

We began to deviate from our original brief of agricultural types and rural craftspeople when other characters with unusual tales captured our imagination. Jo Freestone, for example, with her burlesque dancing, the delightful Ted Ingram – the country's longest serving newspaper deliveryman, Ossie Morris and Graeme Coombs, sadly no longer with us but treasures who will be greatly missed, Clive Farrell with his passion for butterflies, Mark Hix who has built up a chain of London restaurants yet retains strong links with his roots in West Bay. It seemed that Dorset folk could turn their hand to anything and, most importantly, were passionate about the life and work they had chosen. Thus diversity became the theme and we continued our newly-broadened search to include those who were unusual as well as great.

As the book came closer to becoming a reality we were amazed by the coincidences that linked many of those we have included. Acclaimed author Tracy Chevalier was inspired to move to Dorset by her husband's fondness for The Yetties. Jemma Cannon's small skincare shop in Shaftesbury may yet grow to an empire on the scale of Mark Constantine's, which started with one shop in Poole and is now heading for 1,000 outlets globally. Mark is also a keen birdwatcher and his book has been read by our quarryman, Trev Haysom, who shares his ornithological passion. Oxfords bakery has always used Stoate's flour and with their steam oven have links to the Great Dorset Steam Fair. Coincidentally, Ossie Morris is followed alphabetically by Barbara Murray with Ozzy the champion dog. John Morgan has loaned some of his equipment for 'Downton Abbey', the television series created by Lord Fellowes. North Dorset companies Oxfords, Fudges and Dikes have all been linked for generations and are still doing what their forebears set out to do, feeding their happy customers. We have two Cluetts – 'slimey frog name' as described by Malcolm, who do not know each other, but whose resemblance is uncanny.

We thought it best not to pay too much attention to Dr Jane Goodall's flatulent dog, who attempted to dominate our interview, but it made our research ever more entertaining. Dogs, in fact, were in danger of taking over the book as so many of our great faces could not be separated from their canine companions. We have tried to include characters both young and old, male and female, and cover the length and breadth of this stunning county with its geological diversity, as described by Jeremy Pope.

Millie's ability to get the best from her subjects is self-evident, and she has a way of bringing out the twinkle in her subject's eye, not always using conventional methods! We had difficulty gaining entry to the Dorset Fire service HQ, as they were expecting Liz Pope and

Millie Milkington, but after some gentle persuasion we were eventually allocated badges and allowed access. We had other unforgettable moments; photographing Leanne Lady Gaga with her Fame Monsters on Weymouth beach with an audience of old aged pensioners was a definite highlight.

We had to leave out a knots and splices expert, historian, chainsaw artist and many other artists, musicians, chefs and simply fabulous people who we did not have room for, but we enjoyed meeting every single one of them and would like to thank them for giving us their time.

Countless of our interviewees mentioned their love of the coast, the beautiful walks and the fact that there is no motorway in Dorset. Nearly everyone loved the pace of life, the honesty of the people and the fact that many of the old ways haven't changed and hopefully never will.

The whole experience has been life-affirming and has reinforced our view that Dorset is a special and happy place, with friendly, entertaining and successful people, not just in financial terms but in terms of getting the balance right in their lives.

*　　*　　*

We would both like to thank every single person who we have included in this book and those for whom we sadly did not have space. To all those who helped us with tracking people down, making appointments and giving recommendations, we are very grateful. Special gratitude to Etta Stickland for her advice, and Candice Raby for her help with designing the initial layout. Thanks must go to David Burnett at Dovecote Press for believing in this project.

I would like to thank my children, Cosmo Meynell, Louis Pope and Willow Pope for putting up with a busy mother, my father, Patrick Lawrence, for his proof-reading skill and my husband Patrick. Thank you Millie for allowing me to share your dream.

Thank you to all of you who have bought and supported this book. I hope you enjoy it.

LIZ POPE

I would like to thank my mother, Biddy Chittenden, and my husband Ed, for their unerring support and encouragement throughout my career, and my three girls, Daisy, Grace and Flora, who have had to share me, rather more than I would have liked, with my camera. And of course Liz, for helping me bring this project to life.

MILLIE PILKINGTON
Dorset, July 2014

# Kate Adie OBE DL
## Writer and Broadcaster

We received a warm welcome at Kate Adie's Dorset home, which was just the sort of place you'd want to retreat to if you had been somewhere dangerous, exhausting and insalubrious. Although those days are now over for Kate, during her time as Chief News Correspondent for the BBC she did more than her fair share of roughing it. She still works full time; lecturing, writing books and articles, presenting 'From Our Own Correspondent' on Radio 4 twice a week, and is also working on two television documentaries.

Her life so far has certainly been action-packed, though she plays down a lot of it. She claimed she 'got into university by the catflap' because she did no work for A levels and wasn't intending to go to university. However, as it turned out she ended up at Newcastle reading Scandinavian Studies in the 1960s, which she adored. 'It was a new world, it was such fun. We spent our life protesting; hitting people with placards and getting arrested!'

In her early years as a journalist in the 1970s she reported on some landmark moments for women in employment, but it was a world dominated by men. She remembers having to chase the Governor of the Bank of England round his table because he was so horrified to be interviewed by a woman!

Kate told us stories of her time with the BBC, reporting in difficult situations, many of them harrowing. She made light of her experiences, though made it clear that one mustn't confuse an adrenalin rush with excitement. 'You have a job to do – how does a nurse do it?  Does she cry every time someone comes in? It doesn't mean you don't feel about it. It's a tough job, often in difficult situations. If there's aggression, trouble or tension, you mustn't make yourself a target. You mustn't annoy people by just being there to the extent that they will have a go at you or possibly kill you. You also want information from people and they are in a right old state. They may be very angry, furious, full of fear. But you don't want to be a casualty and add to the problem.'

She told us how few people appreciate the work that goes into journalism. During the Bosnian War she once rang her sister from Sarajevo during a five hour shelling. 'I used to have to actually stop on the satphone and say "hang on there's an incoming". I could hear it whistling; there'd be an immense explosion and then it would go quiet and I'd say "There it goes. Hang on." And then you wait ten seconds, because we were very near in and there'd be a great scatter of shrapnel everywhere, and then I'd go on with the conversation. I do remember my sister saying "Are you still alive?" Still alive! At one point I said "We did a good story yesterday. You saw we led the news." And she said, "Yes, it was very short." I said "actually it was one minute and fifty-eight seconds," which was pretty good for the 9 o'clock news, and she said "what did you do for the rest of the day?" And she's not dim! That is the kind of attitude most people have to television, because it looks as if it all just happens in front of the camera.

'It's an iceberg of a job if you do it properly. It consists of hours of travelling in difficult areas, ferreting around, questioning scores of people to try and actually verify something and make sure that you are getting somewhere near an honest version of events – which in conflicts is difficult, because people have good reasons for lying. You spend a lot of time trying to coordinate information before you begin to get a sense of what has really gone on.'

Kate spent seven months with the army in the first Gulf war, and described one terrifying occasion when she was with a group of about 12 journalists, accompanying 7th Armoured Brigade. They were on a desert track through the sand, not tarmac, which hundreds of slow-moving American tanks were using. There were no lights at night, as they were in a combat situation. 'We were in this sort of sand scrape against a dune and we had half erected our tent. We were the worst people – you could always tell where the journalists were – the tent was the sort of collapsed looking one! We'd bedded down for the night, knackered etc, and several of us woke, not me as I'm a heavy sleeper, and heard that tank noise – grinding, squeaking. The next morning we came out and there were people with white faces above us on the top of the sand bank. There were tracks right to the edge of it. An American tank had come up, wandered off the road and overhung us.'

As to the various diseases Kate picked up. 'You try and just keep going. If you can't get water to drink you drink beer. Alcohol never stops in any war zone in the world; it's what fuels soldiers. The brewery in Sarajevo never stopped production. The rest of the town went into medieval meltdown; the only bit of the electricity came from generators and went to the brewery. The water supply was diverted to the brewery.'

After such experiences it's no wonder that Kate chose the peaceful Dorset countryside in which to buy a home. 'I'm a Geordie from the north-east and I'd lived in London for 35 years and wanted to move out, though I still have a flat there, so I thought where to go?' Kate has lots of friends in Dorset, and has recently been appointed one of the county's Deputy Lieutenants, about which she was 'honoured and thrilled'. These days, she finds life in the country so busy she goes to London for a rest!

'You have a job to do – how does a nurse do it? Does she cry every time someone comes in? It doesn't mean you don't feel about it. It's a tough job, often in difficult situations. If there's aggression, trouble or tension, you mustn't make yourself a target.'

The most revolting thing Kate has had to eat is Russian airline food. I suggested sheeps' eyeballs, but she just says no to such things. 'I don't feel any obligation to eat something that's going to make you want to throw up. I don't think it's bad manners. I think it's worse manners to throw up.'

I wondered if there was a highlight to Kate's career, but she described so many places and amazing events where she had seen a country's history change. She recalled the huge crowds in 1989 – tens of thousands of people in Wenceslas Square in Prague – nearly hysterical with hope. 'Were they going to make it this time? Was the Soviet Union going to finally bugger off? Singing all the time. Things like that make the hair rise on the back of your neck.' Or Tianamen Square, where she witnessed a government sending in its own soldiers to kill people. Despite such horrors, Kate is a huge optimist, 'I think people are great. You know the world has a number of bastards, but basically people are good. I am never one to say I wish we could go back to the 18th century. I'd like my teeth please and modern plumbing. I really can't bear the thought. Life gets better – yes it goes two steps forwards, one step back.'

# Mark Anderson
## Sand Sculptor

Twenty odd years ago, Mark was a 22-year-old living with his grandparents and wondering what to do with his life. 'Every morning I used to wake up and think – what would my perfect job involve? – and go through a list of things I wanted; travel, creativity, working outside.' The answer was sand sculpting, something his grandfather, Frank Darrington, had been passionate about since the early 1920s. 'I went downstairs and told my granddad I wanted to be his apprentice.' Mark recalls returning from lunch one day to find the sign reading 'Sand Sculptures by F.G. Darrington' now boasting an attachment, 'and grandson, Mark'. They ended up working together for eight years, travelling abroad to sand sculpting competitions, and Mark is still sculpting now.

The key to success in sand sculpting is in the preparation of the sand and water, usually an 8 to1 ratio, which is then pounded for strength before carving. 96% of Weymouth Beach sand is 0.15 millimetre grain size, which is just bigger than silt and perfect for carving, as each grain has a slight angle to it. A finished sculpture is sprayed with a weather-

proof solution to protect against wind erosion, and some are painted.

For the huge sculptures on display at Lodmoor Country Park, Weymouth, the sand needed by Mark is dumped on site before a marquee is built over the top. It then takes two or three days to prepare the sand for each sculpture and around 12 days to carve, with experts from all over the world flying in to complete the masterpieces. Each year is themed: 'Ancient

Greece,' 'Science Fiction' – this year it is 'Literally Sand', depicting favourite works of fiction. Each sculpture is carefully planned and then built from the top down with the wooden forms, which serve as a platform, removed as the artist works his way to the bottom.

It is a craft best learned through experience, as Mark discovered when attempting a large sculpture of the Venus de Milo in his early days. His grandfather looked on as the sculpture endlessly collapsed with a face that said 'I told you so!' but eventually Mark triumphed, and the six foot tall Aphrodite finally stood firm. It seems you have to be patient and stubborn. Sand World has now been open for four years and, with visitor numbers increasing yearly, it is fast becoming a major Weymouth attraction.

# Emma House and Rae Stormonth-Darling
## The Anonymous Travelling Market

I am sure Emma and Rae of the Anonymous Travelling Market will forgive me for describing them as a little bonkers, in fact they might be disappointed if I didn't. Without their enthusiasm and determination to help local businesses by bringing together a crowd to shop, eat and chat with the hustle and bustle of the community going on around them, life in rural Dorset would be a lot duller. As well as running the actual markets, they arrange live music and are on hand to deal with any quibbles and niggles. Work for Rae, from Iwerne Minster, and Emma, from Shroton, takes up many weekends and whilst most of us are still in bed they are setting up stalls, whatever the weather, and helping their stallholders have a fun and successful day.

A few years ago these two friends, who have four daughters and a step-daughter between them, started making slabs of fudge, which they sold locally. This led them to thinking, whilst walking on Hambledon Hill, that local makers and craftspeople needed an arena to help sell their wares. Inspiration struck and The Anonymous Travelling Market was born.

Now they have a pool of around 200 stallholders to draw on for their markets, tailoring the stalls to the likely visitors and putting on about 25 markets a year. Some are in High Streets, others at various fairs, yet more in the gardens of private houses such as Deans Court and Waterstone Manor. This summer they joined forces with the Spring Tide Food Festival, hosted by the National Trust on Burton Bradstock beach.

Stalls with the ATM include a South American Chicken Bus, coffee sellers, cheesemakers, clothes sellers, chutney producers, and wood crafts. Emma and Rae themselves dabble in hair garlands, fabric flowers, fudge, and a 'paint your pants' stall, when they have a moment between setting up the markets and looking after the other sellers and musicians. 'Music is absolutely crucial,' Rae tells me, 'it makes people happy and relaxed and then they stay longer.' It also plays a vital role in supporting local talent, and The Blackmore Vale Dairy sponsors the music tent at some of their events.

Emma admits that they didn't have much idea what they were doing when they started in 2009. 'It was slightly fraught for us, because we didn't know the rhythm of it. If you have a stallholder sitting like a crab at the back of their stall you have to encourage them out.' Since then they have become adept at setting up and, most importantly, making visitors feel welcome. Emma explains, 'You are wearing pretty stupid clothes so if something does begin to kick off, they see me in a pink negligee or Rae covered in flowers, then it slightly defuses what might be a tricky situation.' They both have a great spirit and sense of humour, not to mention infectious laughs.

Despite having families to look after, Emma also teaches and runs 'Emma & the Magic Bag' a high-octane and entertaining music class for babies and toddlers. Rae sighed, 'It's the after bit that's harder to recover from.' They have often helped set up 30 stalls on Saturday and 30 on Sunday, so by Monday they are completely shattered. 'We are talking to each and every stallholder and putting on a lovely smile, and beefing them up and you've the wind and the rain or the sun, and by the end of it you feel like you've been up a mast in a Force 10 gale!'

Rae and Emma are also keen to encourage the younger generation to get involved. They ran a Young Entrepreneurs competition which involved inviting primary school children to send in their ideas for a stall that would raise money for their PTA. The winning school now has a stall selling its own stationery.

Inevitably, despite their efforts at marketing and publicity, sometimes things are a little slow. If this happens Emma and Rae have been known to turn to gymnastics to jolly things along. Even if the local produce doesn't tempt you, surely the possibility of catching a couple of eccentrically attired ladies doing star jumps for your amusement might get you to grab your purse and rush down to their next market – who knows, you might even join in!

# Richard Balson
## Master Butcher

Balson Butchers was established in 1515 when Henry VIII was on the throne, and has occupied the same premises in Bridport since 1880. There's been the odd black sheep in the family and sometimes it has switched to a brother's son, but otherwise the family firm has passed from father to son for 28 generations. Unsurprisingly, it is justly celebrated as England's oldest family business.

Richard Balson explains how things have changed over the years. 'When I first started you only had beef sausages and pork sausages now there are 20 – kangaroo, cranberry, wild boar, venison . . . People buy less big joints now, they want what they can cook quickly. With all these cookery programmes on the telly you'd think people would be a bit more savvy, more aware of different things to do. But the modern housewife – and I'm not being detrimental – if they can't put it in a microwave they don't bloody want it! Ovens have got smaller, you wouldn't get a 20 pound turkey in most of them like you would in the old days.'

It's not all bad though. Balsons sell a lot of game, which is good for health and good for the countryside.

Richard doesn't mess with words, a true Dorset man who gets straight to the point. 'My son is in London but he'll come into the family business,' he told me.

'Would you mind if he didn't?'

'Well he'd be shot!'

# Richard Batterham
## Potter

'Are you still learning?' I asked. Richard chuckled, 'still making a hell of a lot of mistakes!'

Having had the pleasure of meeting Richard Batterham, widely regarded as one of the most respected potters working today, I have re-evaluated my relationship with pottery, in particular the everyday items used for eating and drinking.

Each piece that Richard makes is unique and something to be cherished. He thinks the word functional is somehow derogatory when it comes to describing his pieces, or their use. 'If it is just a jug or a mug, if it doesn't do what people look for in a unique piece, then it's not really functioning. Just to have a mug, just to have a thing with a handle that you can drink out of, that's not really enough. You expect all the things that go into making a nice pot, the feel, the weight, as if it was an individual piece.'

His whole being seems absorbed in his work and he savours the best pieces that come out of each firing, taking them over the road from his studio to his house, for his personal use. People occasionally break something, he told us, be it a mug or a pot and think, oh well, plenty more where that came from but Richard doesn't agree. Those were the special pieces, selected by him, for his home, and each pot has meaning. 'After a while they are the ones you always do this with, or the one you always make that with, or that was so and so's when she was a little girl.'

Bryanston School, Don Potter, produced a beautiful stone carving over the front door proclaiming 'Richard Batterham 1966'. There is an immaculately tended vegetable patch at the back and he can't remember ever having to buy vegetables. The fishmonger dropped by whilst we were there and Richard nipped out to get some fresh prawns and crab.

His dusty and cobwebbed studio – where bowls of walnuts, gathered but uneaten, have become still lives – has a woodburner with a simple but inviting wooden chair and a footstool. Richard smiled, 'I would never put my feet up!' whilst admitting that he does sit down a lot more than he used to; understandable at 78 years old.

Richard moved to Durweston as the clay he uses comes from not far away in Wareham and he had happy childhood memories of Dorset, but wasn't keen on being near the coast with its crowds of summer visitors. He describes Dorset as having 'been kind' and 'it's just where it is – it's just comfortable.'

'Do you give talks?' I asked.

'Talks? No, no I don't talk. I don't teach either. I'm a bit dubious about people being taught. There's too much of, so and so was trained by this and that; I think people should learn. If you are taught then you are taught to do what somebody else is doing. If you learn, you learn what you need to learn and what you need to know.'

'Are you still learning?' I asked.

Richard chuckled, 'still making a hell of a lot of mistakes!'

Richard works alone with no help. Pottery can be highly physically demanding. 'You have to work hard – hell of a lot of pots – if you make a living you have to.'

Cheekily I asked if he would ever retire. 'What? To do what I want to do you mean?'

From my perspective, they are most definitely not just pots, but items that have become interwoven into his life and, I imagine he hopes, the lives of the people he sells to.

He appears to live the most idyllic and simple life in Durweston, uncluttered by any trait of greed or vanity. He does not sign his work and it tickles him that this confounds the so called experts and dealers, who cannot draw comfort from a mark or signature to signify the provenance of a piece.

I was amazed at this lack of possessiveness over his work. 'The short answer is it doesn't make the pots any better. If you put "me, me, me" on the bottom of everything, then it's being very sort of egotistical, but if you are just making pots, or doing anything, and you are just doing it, it's actually much more – it's got "you" out of the way. When you are making pots you make hundreds of them and all the time to be putting "me, me, me" is too much.'

He works in a studio that is pretty much unchanged since it was purpose built, on the site of the old Durweston Church. His mentor and teacher at

# Jim Bettle
## Charcoal Burner

You can't hurry a charcoal burn. Patience is required to get perfect results. As Jim Bettle said, 'Try and rush any stage of it and it comes back to bite you!' But charcoal burning can involve being in a birdsong-filled wood, perhaps getting on with a bit of coppicing for the next batch, so it is not too difficult to wait for the steel kiln to work its magic.

Jim started the Dorset Charcoal Company around 17 years ago, now producing up to 30 tonnes of charcoal a year and, with the help of two lads, firing his kilns from late February to November.

The initial fire is started from the middle and spreads from the centre outwards. Sticks are laid on the bottom as runners, carrying a channel into the middle, together with a little pile of charcoal from the previous burn. Then a raft of hardwood is built over the top making a flat level, with some brash or light incendiary material, as a spreading layer, with the timber piled on top. The thinner, drier wood is put to the edge, the coldest part of the kiln. Thus everything has been built up round a chimney, leaving an access hole to a pile of charcoal where embers are introduced to start the fire. In time, 12-24 hours depending on the greenness of the wood, and with the correct restriction of the oxygen supply, charcoal will be produced.

Jim has lived in Dorset all his life. He is passionate about his work and champions the cause of coppicing and maintaining woods in an environmentally sound way. He helped found the Dorset Coppice Group, which educates adults and children about coppicing, hurdle-making, charcoal production and other aspects of forestry. Jim feels education is the key. For nightingales, butterflies and woodland flowers to thrive woods require seasonal cutting and opening up of the forest floor. 'The only way it is going to get done is if there's a market for the products.'

As well as charcoal for cooking, he also produces softwood bark free charcoal briquettes, for laboratories to test fire retardancy on furniture, train seats etc. Every size has a use and none is wasted. Finer charcoal is graded, with the finest powder going for cosmetics, and larger grades for animal feed, garden additives, and so on. He has produced charcoal for the Prince of Wales at Highgrove and the Chelsea Flower Show.

# Jez Bragg
## Ultra Distance Runner

If I asked you 'Which is your favourite run in Dorset?' I'd put money on you not giving me the answer Jez Bragg gave, 'Oh, probably Poole to Weymouth, along the coast path.' That's about 34 miles!

Jez is now in his early thirties but looks at least a decade younger. At school and university he played rugby and has always kept physically active. Aged 20 he trained for a marathon to raise money for charity and this led him on to ultra running (anything longer than a marathon, or 26.2 miles). In reality, the shortest standard distance considered an ultra is 50 kilometres, or 31.07 miles. Other standard distances are the 50 mile, 100 mile, 100 km, and a series of events that last for specified time periods such as 6 hour, 12 hour, 24 hour, 48 hour, and 6 days.

Jez was attracted to this endurance sport because he loves the outdoors and the chance to reach places most others can't. He owes his inner strength, which is vital, to his upbringing.

He doesn't listen to music whilst running, as 'that makes you aware of time – you know an album is roughly an hour. You want to slot into a sustainable rhythm, hour after hour, that's the trick.'

All this running, with no distractions is, as Jez puts it 'an incredible opportunity to explore in a pure way. I love the network of footpaths (in Dorset)' and it would seem he has run them all.

Imagine the rough, remote, boggy and mountainous terrain of New Zealand. Imagine setting out to run from the top of North Island to the bottom of South Island, using a kayak to cross the Cook Strait. This is the Te Araroa trail which is 1,898 miles in length. Jez Bragg, the face of UK ultra running for his outstanding achievements, completed this in late 2013 in a mere 53 days, which meant running 12-16 hours each day.

Jez does describe himself as a fitness freak and also admits that he's not that impressed with his best marathon time of 2 hours and 42 minutes.

In 2010 he won the Ultra-Trail du Mont-Blanc (7 valleys, 71 glaciers, 400 summits), but on the world stage the run he would ideally like to improve on is his third position in the Western States Endurance Run (100 miles across California). He would also like to

tackle the Mount Fiji trail (97 miles) in Japan. So much to look forward to!

Jez's mental attitude is evidently key in these tests of endurance and he says he is 'stubborn, competitive and determined'. When he sets out to do something, he does it. He also loves the mountain craft of these challenges – when to eat, knowing what is manageable, staying safe – basic survival really. In the world of elite sports, ultra running is gathering pace and Jez's sponsors, North Face, have latched onto this and are keen to encourage others who want to challenge themselves – which is what Jez Bragg does so well.

# Robert Braithwaite
## Boat Builder, Founder of Sunseeker International Ltd

Rumour has it that Daniel Craig was not unduly keen when he heard that Robert Braithwaite was going to be driving the Sunseeker Sovereign 17 foot in a James Bond 007 movie. But Robert's easy manner, open face and candid smile soon won over the British star. Robert was warned that he might not get a great reception. 'I thought, right when I meet him [Craig], I'll say yes sir, no sir, which I do anyway. Pretence is nothing to me – I'm an ordinary guy and why shouldn't I be?'

Despite his modesty, Robert is something of a legend in the world of international boatbuilding. He has been involved with boats since he was 14 and now, past the age of normal retirement, he is President of a global brand turning over hundreds of millions of pounds, employing around 5,000 people. Sunseeker was sold in 2013 to a Chinese consortium but it remains firmly based in Dorset.

When Robert started the business in the 1960s, John, his brother who is five years younger, was still in school. 'Unfortunately we lost our parents early. That's one of these things that happens in life, so I had to bring him up. John wasn't interested in the commercial side of the business but he liked designing so he still runs the design centre with 60 people in it. No-one else in the marine business has a design centre like that.'

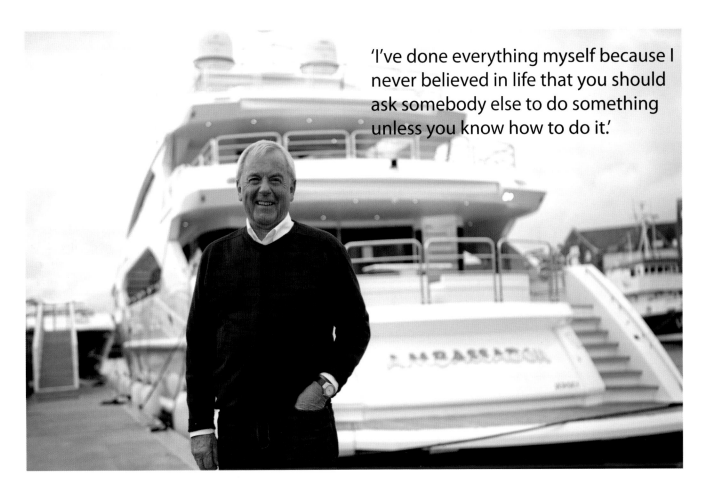

'I've done everything myself because I never believed in life that you should ask somebody else to do something unless you know how to do it.'

For the James Bond films, Sunseeker provides two boats to keep them running and a shell to blow up. 'What that did for us was make us a household name in Australia, America and China. I always wanted to create a name that was like Hoover.'

'The biggest thing I enjoyed was when I worked on the shop floor, because building the product I worked down there with the men, drove the forklift, tested the boats, built the boats. I've done everything myself because I never believed in life that you should ask somebody else to do something unless you know how to do it.'

From the rich and famous clients who demand the best, to the dusty workmen in high visibility jackets in the boatyard, who call him boss, shake his hand warmly and tell him how well he looks, Robert has a way with people. In a crisp white shirt, navy jersey and jeans he looks relaxed, whilst the zing of entering the yard and seeing these white beasts rising up from

their moulds is something he is passionate about. The biggest boat to be produced by Sunseeker yet, at 155 feet, just under 500 tonnes, is poking out of a shed which will have to be extended to accommodate it, as it is being built for a long-standing client whose boats have simply got bigger and bigger.

'You do need a car but you don't need a boat,' Robert told us, so what they've always tried to do is create a dream. The big problem they had in the early days was the ladies! 'You've created this brand. Men loved it but had to convince their wives, so we had to get designers into the interiors to help us make the boats more feminine. That's been the challenge. We've been very lucky to do that. People knew exactly what it was when they saw a Sunseeker and that's one reason why we've carried on being successful, because we created a global brand. You wouldn't be successful otherwise in today's world.'

# Russell Brown
## Chef proprietor, Sienna Restaurant

When Russell Brown gave up smoking in his late twenties his appetite returned. He started cooking more seriously, prompting him to get a job in a commercial kitchen in Cornwall where he learned the craft skills of excellent cuisine – the rest, as the cliché goes, is history.

As we sit in his tiny Dorchester restaurant (it seats a maximum of fifteen), he talks of seared scallops, handmade agnolotti, sweetcorn velouté, and although it is only 9.30 in the morning, we are salivating. With an intelligent approach to his cooking and a calm, controlled and relaxed kitchen staff preparing vegetables in the background, he is obviously proud of his three rosettes from the AA and his Michelin star – the only restaurant in Dorset to have one.

Now in its tenth year, Sienna, named after the colour, not the Italian city, is thriving. The choice of name was not easy. 'Finding the name for a restaurant is a nightmare. There is a requirement from a practical point of view to have something that is short and reasonably easy for people to say, not something they can't pronounce and are then embarrassed about.' His wife, Eléna, who works front of house, came up with Sienna, which ties in well with their surname, Brown. Russell also enjoys the culinary joke that you get both burnt and raw sienna, so it stuck.

'We've always tried to serve great food, a really interesting wine list to go with it but in a nice relaxed atmosphere. There is no great formality – there are no tablecloths on the tables. Eléna will pour your wine when you order it but then she leaves the bottle on the table for you to help yourself.'

'If I have a passion for anything particular it is probably pastry, and if somebody said you have to choose a section in the kitchen to run forever that is what I would go for, though I wouldn't want to make

the choice. We try very hard to make sure the quality is even across the whole of the meal, from the *petit fours* to the bread to the canapés, right the way through all the different courses. No one thing should stand out as being wow! Everything should be of a level.

'What we do is about the ingredients and the seasonality and is generally classic combinations, not about pushing the envelope in the sense of trying to

come up with weird and wonderful new things.'

Russell believes the key to excellent cooking is taste, 'being able to make a judgement as to whether a dish is correctly seasoned, and whether it balances. You have to teach young chefs to taste, not to eat, and there is a big difference between those two. You have to learn to think about what you are eating and concentrate on it.'

The Browns have lived in Dorset for just over a decade. 'I've probably never lived more than 20 miles from the coast, and can't imagine not living close to the sea.' If Russell had time for a walk, when not cooking for his restaurant or doing charity demonstrations, he'd go along the cliffs from Burton Bradstock, no doubt pondering the next dish with which to enthrall his fortunate diners.

'I am very bad at delegating, so I find if someone is going to make a mistake I'd rather it was me. By the time you've told someone what to do it takes forever to put it right.'

# Tanya Bruce-Lockhart
## Festival Organiser

By her own admission, Tanya Bruce-Lockhart has a low boredom threshold. 'That's why I do festivals,' she told us. One festival isn't enough to keep her occupied so she organises two. The Beaminster Music Festival in the summer, and the Bridport Literary Festival in the autumn.

When she first moved to Beaminster from London, thirteen years ago, she decided she didn't want to take up gardening or play bridge, and, as she puts it, she doesn't kill things, so organising cultural events and bringing people together was what she chose. I imagine there are countless people in West Dorset who bless the day Tanya, and her extensive address book, arrived. Having worked in television for many years she was able to attract some well known musicians and writers, which combined with her huge personality undoubtedly contributed to her success.

'You do it because you enjoy doing it but also because it's a contribution to the community. Most of the people who come are appreciative and say so, but there are inevitably those who take you for granted and think that you are going to do it forever and a day, and don't really understand how it all comes together. I find that sometimes I get a bit hypersensitive about it. Some people are wonderfully eulogistic. Others are sort of whingers because they want more Baroque!

'I am very bad at delegating, so I find if someone is going to make a mistake I'd rather it was me. By the time you've told someone what to do it takes forever to put it right. I have an army of helpers for Beaminster, doing budgets, and a committee.' Sadly, she feels this year will be her last, but hopes someone else will take it on. 'Once I hand it over,' she says, 'it has to be somebody else's vision.' She does all the fundraising for Beaminster herself and imagines her friends see her coming and thinking, 'Oh God, what money does she want now!'

Tanya claims to have two obsessions, books and rhinos. The house is full to bursting with both. Piles of books line the stairs and her library is stuffed. Rhinos in every medium adorn walls, shelves, corners – she is indiscriminate in her collecting and feels them to be misunderstood, vulnerable creatures.

Another clear obsession is dogs. She has had many rescue animals and the current incumbent, a soppy Staffordshire bull terrier, called Lily, was enchanting. Such is her love of all things canine that she nearly resigned her job over a previous pet. She was working at London Weekend Television with the late Frank Muir when she was told she was not allowed to bring her dog to work, so told Frank she would have to leave. Frank wasn't having any of this and wrote to the chairman explaining the importance of Tanya Bruce-Lockhart's dog. 'She imported this animal from southern Spain believing it to be of canine extraction and when she introduced it to her vet he pronounced it as a very rare species of hornless Andalucian goat, and there's nothing in the working association of London Weekend Television to say she may not have a goat!' All Tanya's contracts from then on were written 'Tanya Bruce-Lockhart and the goat, Ricky', which she thought was a good wheeze!

# William Bryer
## Master of Foxhounds

Will Bryer made sure we were ready before he let the hounds out of their kennels. They were mad with excitement and he was only just managing to hold them back at the door as we braced ourselves for the outpouring of muscle, slavering chops and raw enthusiasm. A few gentle taps and sharp words were all that were needed however, to keep these powerful creatures at bay, and stop them from knocking us over in their bid to gain affection.

The oldest Cattistock line goes back to an Irish bitch called 'Limerick Waspish 1874' who came over from Ireland. Every hound has its own character. 'Chalice 09' (denoting the year it starts work not the year of birth) is a particular favourite of Will's for her remarkable hunting ability. Those invisible characteristics of nose, tongue (voice), stamina, drive and intelligence are most important; whilst good conformation is vital for longevity of working life.

The hounds are exercised daily in the summer, initially on foot, then bicycle from May, then finally horse before the start of the hunting season. Their obedience is conditioned through this exercise and they are introduced to the outside world of cars, dog walkers, cats, cattle, sheep and obstacles to cross, jump and squeeze through. This prepares young hounds, with older hounds acting as mentors, as well as building the bond between hounds and huntsman, and hardening their pads and muscle in an effort to keep them strong for winter. Injuries caused by barbed wire and blackthorn are always a threat.

Work is something at which hounds excel, running up to 40 miles a day for 70-80 days in a season. Will tells me, 'they are super tough and rarely unable to stick the rigours of a day, returning, like the horses, tired but happy.'

In 2001 Will went to County Limerick in Ireland to hunt hounds. Coincidentally the oldest unbroken Limerick line of hounds goes back to the same bitch, 'Limerick Waspish'. At the time there was a lot of public animosity towards hunting in England. By the date of his return in 2010 this had eased, and people are now generally more aware of how inclusive hunting is. Since the ban (which came into force in February 2005) he feels that attitudes are a good deal more positive and the publicity surrounding foxhunting has opened it up to a greater understanding. 'I have never met a hunting person yet who does not love and care for their animals, tame or wild – and their rural environment. That speaks volumes to me.'

Will Bryer has ridden all his life, his mother Jinks is a well known Dorset horsewoman who has taught countless people to ride, and horses are well and truly in his blood. So it is no great surprise that having hunted all over Ireland, he was invited to return to Dorset as Joint Master and huntsman of the Cattistock in 2010.

The Cattistock Hunt was founded in the 18th century and originally known as the True Blue Hunt, which explains why they now wear blue coats, with a small splash of red, harking back to those scarlet days. As Master, Will organises the running of the country and the kennels. His perk, as he sees it, is hunting the hounds because that is what he first fell in love with.

Will was keen to stress the importance of hunting to the rural community and how intertwined the hunt is to the farming side of country life. The Cattistock Hunt Skittles League is a good example of how, over many generations, hunting has enmeshed itself into the countryside. Playing skittles provides an opportunity for the rural community to get together throughout the winter and play against a different team each week, which means farmers get to meet up and exchange ideas.

Will described how 'hunting a pack of hounds and being allowed to cross farms through the sporting goodwill of farmers is a tremendous and unique privilege, so, with that in mind, every day should be considered a good day. Obviously some are better than others but a huntsman is always trying to produce one of those really magic days where hounds run and run.

It's the most wonderful thing to witness, a pack in full cry streaming across the country. Add to this a horse and the challenge of riding behind the hounds at full tilt; the stresses of normal life are left far behind.

'My idea of a good day might be different to someone else's. For some, the chance to jump a row of hedges at a strong gallop is their thing, but for me, whilst I love my horses, the hound work is supreme. There is huge variety because it's that sort of a sport; it is inclusive because people can enjoy it on so many different levels. Foot followers, landowners, kids out hunting who often have parents who are new to riding – it brings together a huge diversity of people from everywhere. Never do you get such a good cross section of society anywhere else.'

Of Dorset Will says, 'We are still a rural county blessed not to have a motorway. We are the lucky ones, working in a place with such a stunningly beautiful backdrop.' He admires the farming community, who he describes as hugely sporting with a lovely generous side to them. 'We enjoy great support from nearly 600 landowners and farmers. There is a real *esprit de corps* here in West Dorset amongst those of us determined to maintain our heritage – and for many of us, hunting lies at its core.'

Will has to confess that he is biased. He was born and raised here and now lives only a mile down the road from where his life began.

# Rob Buckley
## Dorset Centre for Rural Skills

With an enviable view of Hambledon Hill, Rob and Susie Buckley work and live in rural bliss. They set up the Dorset Centre for Rural Skills (DCRS) ten years ago when they realised that many of the old rural crafts were in danger of dying out. They had long employed traditional techniques to restore ancient buildings and were determined to pass the skills they had acquired on to others, to keep them alive.

They offer courses in welding, straw bale house-building, lime rendering, glass blowing, black-smithing, and stone carving – as well as traditional rural crafts such as hedge laying, hurdle making, and chair bodging. Some of the disciplines are taught by Rob, but where necessary local craftsmen are brought in to pass on their knowledge.

They teach anyone who wants to learn, from the course 'junkies', as they call those who are seemingly addicted to learning, to those who are 'fed up with driving a keyboard every day' and who want to do something practical. They have also worked with the Prince's Trust helping young men and women get back into work. Rob explains, 'They'd come here with very low self-esteem, then learn a skill over a couple of weeks and suddenly they'd change completely and think, "Perhaps I'm not so useless."'

Eight years ago Rob set up a sister company, DCRS Construction, which specialises in sustainable new build houses as well as traditional renovation. Using all the skills taught by DCRS the construction company combines modern technology with traditional methods to create low energy, highly insulated buildings.

Rob's loves his life in Dorset but, like many country-men has a mixed view on those who only come down for the weekend to their country cottage. 'They do bring money and wealth in, which if they spend locally is great, and to a certain extent they tend to preserve historic buildings. But equally this pushes up prices so local people can't buy. It has got to a point where whole villages have lost their heart. But when you get to the other side of Iwerne Minster – out here – in what we call deepest darkest Dorset and further on, towards Marnhull and all the way out in the Blackmore Vale, that is sort of a bit untouched because it's a bit scary for them! They think ooh they've got webbed feet and six toes out there!'

# Don Byfleet
## Morris Dancer

Don Byfleet proudly announced that he is eighty-eight and three-quarters. He was born in 1926 and had to ask me what year it was now. When we'd worked out his age he exclaimed 'I'm ancient, but my brother is 92!'

You can also forgive him for not having made it up to the top of Giant Hill in Cerne Abbas to join his fellow Morris Men for their annual May Day dance at sunrise. Instead, Don waited at the bottom for the procession to the Cerne Abbas pubs for the inevitable merry making and dancing.

Don has been a Morris man since 1948 when he was 'dragooned into it by a Scout group!' The Wessex Morris Men were formed in 1956 and it was in 1977, on the first May Day Bank Holiday, that Don conceived the idea of holding an annual May morning dance. The old maypole site above the Cerne Giant's head seemed the appropriate place.

Was there anywhere you'd still like to dance? I asked him. 'If there was, I'd have danced it!' he said.

Morris dancing can be traced back to the mid 15th century. The Wessex Morris men is an all male team, dancing mainly in the Cotswold tradition. They are also an active member of the Morris Ring, which was formed eighty years ago to encourage the performance of the Morris, to maintain its traditions and to preserve its history. They dance mainly in the late spring and summer, often at local shows, fêtes and other public events and can be booked for private parties.

Was there anywhere you'd still like to dance? I asked him. 'If there was, I'd have danced it!' he said.

# Jemma Cannon
## Herbalist and Soap Maker

In a green shed in her parents' paddock in Buckhorn Weston, Jemma, who did a degree in Medicinal Plants, followed by an advisory role at Neal's Yard Remedies, cooks up her soaps and other skincare products in the most traditional way. The soaps are cured for six weeks and not sold until they are set, which is weather dependent, then they are packaged, labelled and taken to Jemma's beautifully scented, Shaftesbury shop.

Jemma radiates health and wholesomeness and with her perfect skin and winning smile it isn't hard to see how you could be won over by her products. The fact that they are organic and handmade from only the best materials, 'no sulphates, no nasties', bears out her passion for her craft. Customers have been known to get frustrated by having to wait for perfect ingredients to be sourced; Jemma will not settle for anything less. Her hand lotion, with its organic flax seed oil and cocoa butter, simply melts into the skin.

'Everything we do is plant-based and I love putting it all together. The nicest thing is that we have such a following locally. I get asked about medical things and have people who've been coming for years. It makes it all worthwhile, because you see them improve over the months.' With such a passion for producing honest products, Enchanted Plants has the potential to grow into a multinational chain. This book shares its pages with another business that had humble beginnings making skincare products in one small Dorset location (*see Mark Constantine, page 48*).

Jemma has a true belief in what she does and her enthusiasm for sharing that knowledge is a rarity in a highly competitive market. Such integrity is increasingly hard to find. But for Jemma it is all rather simple, after all, 'Life's only one shot isn't it?'

# Fanny Charles
## Journalist

'Madonna used to shop in Gillingham, we all saw her in Waitrose, but nobody ever hassled her. That's a bit Dorset. I'd hate it to change.'

I doubt Fanny Charles needs much introduction. She was editor of the *Blackmore Vale Magazine* for 22 years, set up the Taste of Dorset Awards, of which she is particularly proud, and is a stalwart of Dorset community life.

Originally a journalist on the *Western Gazette* she moved to the *Blackmore Vale Magazine* in the 1980s. Since then the magazine has grown into one of the icons of life in the south west and its wide readership look forward to poring over it every Friday morning. 'It is universally known as the Bible,' she tells us, 'and we had to look surprised if someone told us they called it the Blessed Virgin Mary, even though we had lost count of the number of times someone had said that!'

Her time at the BVM meant a great deal to Fanny and she is proud of the team she ran there. It is apparently still surprising to some people to find a woman editor, Fanny said, relating an encounter with a District Councillor who refused to believe she was the editor of the most influential magazine in his constituency. Fanny left the BVM in September 2013 and the magazine is now changing to meet a more commercial market.

Fanny is a member of the Guild of Food writers. She is a regular judge for the Great Taste Awards and one of the founders of the Dorset Festival at Poundbury, which started in 2012 as a one off for the Olympics, and was such a success it has carried on. She is also one of the founders of Screenbites – the country's only film and food festival which takes place in the autumn. Fanny was also Chairman of Chalk and Cheese Local Action Group, which works with local people and businesses to develop opportunities for improving the quality of rural life, at the same time as contributing to the local economy.

Fanny is now co-editor of The Fine Times Recorder,

reporting on local foods and the visual arts. The FTR, published weekly, is described as an e-emporium of information on how you might spend your free time in Dorset, Somerset and beyond.

On Dorset, Fanny is as effusive as anyone who has lived or worked here most of their life. She loves the fact that Dorset doesn't have a motorway and is not a primary tourist destination. 'Dorset people are not a bunch of hay seeds, no matter what people who live within the magic circle of the M25 think!'

# Ivor Charles
## Retired Fisherman and Actor

Ivor Charles was waiting patiently for us outside the King's Arms in Weymouth. The moment we saw him we understood why he's appeared in countless films, as an extra portraying a classic fisherman.

Waiting at the King's Arms wasn't too much of a hardship for Ivor, as it is 'headquarters', with the Duke of Cornwall running a close second. Both are where he likes to go dancing, his eyes twinkling as he explains that he can then dance with much younger women – he is 75 after all. 'My mum taught me to dance, to waltz, when I was three, standing on 'er feet and I've danced all the other dances in between including that twist – I 'ate that bloomin' thing – 'orrible. Like I say I've learned to dance with ladies.'

Now retired from fishing, Ivor still goes out on his boat *Humdinger*, and is very much part of the Weymouth fishing community. He told us he has negative buoyancy so he can't swim.

The idea of becoming a film extra was first put to him by a friend who suggested he signed up with an agency. They recognised his potential instantly and he has not been short of work, with credits including 'The Boat that Rocked', 'Cinderella', 'Snow White and the Henchman'.

An ex-Coldstream Guardsman, Ivor is unsurprisingly known as the Captain; a tribute both to his profession and resemblance to the star of the Birds' Eye fish finger ads from the late 1960s. He is keen on his new film career. Although he loves fishing and one can't imagine this salty sea dog – in his words 'more salty than sea dog' – away from water, he is hoping more parts will come his way. He wouldn't mind playing Captain Birdseye, 'Look I'm the slimmer, trimmer version. I'm the healthy option! 'Cos he was a big fat fella wasn't 'e.'

In a drama series called 'da Vinci's Demons' he and the other fishermen were asked if they minded handling fish. Ivor said, 'I can gut it, skin it, fillet it, do whatever you want with it!' They brought him a ling and he dealt with it and they said 'Oh, for the film could you do it slower?' 'So I'm doing it in bloody slow motion and I said, I might need another fish 'cos they're doing all these retakes and the bloody thing's falling apart! I got £30 for talking and an extra £30 for gutting and filleting – brilliant result! I done thousands of fish and never got paid 30 quid for it. Brilliant, love it!'

We had a lovely time with Ivor and I can easily imagine his acting career taking off. In the meantime, and before he gets too busy, he did wonder if I'd like to mention that he's single and available! Don't take him away from Dorset and its blue sea though – he loves them too much.

# Tracy Chevalier
## Writer

'There are no hills so big  you can't walk up them and I like that. You are very snug in Dorset, I feel this valley holds me and I feel part of the landscape.'

On a scorching July day we sat in Tracy's idyllic garden in the Piddle Valley and listened to her chat, from the heart it seemed, on why she loves Dorset and what moved her into buying a house here ten years ago. Tracy is as engaging with her talking as she is with her writing. In her captivating American accent (she is orginally from Washington DC), she extolled the virtues of Dorset living.

Tracy wanted to be a writer or a librarian as a child because she loved books so much. She studied literature at university and then went into publishing, writing short stories on the side. The worldwide success of her second novel *Girl with a Pearl Earring*, which has so far sold 4 million copies, allowed her to become a full time novelist.

'I first got to know Dorset when in around 1990 John (her husband) said "Let's go to Dorset as I know it. Let's go to Yetminster – that's where the Yetties are from!"' They found a lovely B&B and ended up going back year after year because they had such a great time. The sheepdog from the B&B followed them around, and they enjoyed walking through the village to get the paper. All good country experiences!

'As an American I am used to "Trespassers will be Shot!" So you don't go on their property. But with public rights of way it's a completely new experience to be able to cross someone's farm. It really opens up the countryside to you so you can get embedded in it – it's not held off, so I felt immediately that Dorset is really accessible and I love it because it is so human-size; I love the scale of it. There are no hills so big you can't walk up them and I like that. You are very snug in Dorset. I feel this valley holds me and I feel part of the landscape. I like being in the view – it's just fabulous. The other thing I love about Dorset is that there is no motorway!'

Coming to Dorset is time out for Tracy and she tries just to relax when she's here. 'It's ironic as I set stuff down here,' she explains. 'Three of my books have Dorset connections and yet I try not to write here if possible.' In *Burning Bright* one of the families comes from Piddletrenthide so there are lots of references to the Piddle Valley. *Remarkable Creatures* is a novel about Mary Anning so that is set almost entirely in Lyme Regis, and *The Last Runaway* is about a character from Bridport.

For someone so successful Tracy was refreshingly down to earth, admitting that 'we humans have a hard time finishing things. It's easy to start something and very hard to finish it!'

We spent a lovely morning with her and she could not have been more accommodating, even clearing away the cat's dead mice from the lawn before we arrived. With her remarkable patience I am sure she will enjoy many happy decades of Dorset life, at a Dorset pace.

# Terry Clapp
## Fire Fighter

Terry is the station manager at West Moors training centre in Ferndown. He remembers being given a fireman's cap as a small child and wearing it whilst smoking his grandfather's pipe, so it seems he was destined to become a fireman. He is the fourth generation of his family to serve as a fire fighter, beginning with his great grandfather, Harry Birch.

As station manager Terry is responsible for training all operational personnel. Before this current role he was station commander at Springbourne and Westbourne stations in Bournemouth.

The Dorset Fire and Rescue service has 26 fire stations across Dorset, Bournemouth and Poole (they are listed as separate areas as they are run by different fire authorities). Main headquarters is at Poundbury, just outside Dorchester. It responds to over 8,500 incidents each year and has statutory responsibilities for fire safety prevention, attendance at road accidents and attending major incidents – such as flooding or those that involve chemical, biological, radiological, nuclear and explosive hazards. There are 40 fire engines, most of which are crewed by retained duty staff, such as Terry, who are paid on a pay as you go basis for training and fire calls. The annual budget to run the county service is £30 million, 40% of which comes from the government and the rest from council tax.

As you can imagine from such a vital public service role, Terry has been in some interesting situations, the most unusual of which was being called out to rescue a budgie which had flown down a pipe and under the floorboards. Compressed air down the pipe failed to flush the distressed bird out but did produce a few feathers. It was decided amongst Terry and his colleagues that the floorboards would have to come up and underneath they discovered the rather startled creature hard pressed against a grill, but luckily still perky.

He's had near escapes from buildings on fire and his excellent training and good judgement have obviously kept him and many others alive and able to continue with their objectives, 'to save life, property and render humanitarian aid.'

# John Cluett
## Railway Enthusiast, Musician and Artist

You could be forgiven for thinking you'd arrived in the Christmas elves' workshop when you turn up to meet John Cluett, this imposing, true Dorset man. He was tapping away in his garage, skillfully making model trains, tracks, and all sorts of bits and pieces out of unwanted scraps. He has a gauge 1 model railway running the length of his garden.

With his friendly chat, interspersed with an 'Ooh aye' in a broad Dorset accent, John described his days as a lorry driver and working as a signalman on the Somerset and Dorset Railway. Now retired, John's many hobbies keep him busy and active. He makes cider, and with his wife Margaret makes up the folk duo 'Tatty Bogle'. He is also a keen painter and has recently exhibited at Shaftesbury Arts Centre. Though

he now lives in Shaftesbury, John was born and bred in Sturminster Newton and speaks true dialect, rare to hear these days. There are many Cluetts in the area who must be related, but connections have now been lost. John did not know of Malcolm, the farmer from Lydlinch who follows John on the next page.

Dressed in a bright pink tie, jazzy waistcoat and a hat, which he is rarely without, he serenaded us in his garage, with his folk songs and jaunty tunes. The music wafted through the streets and brought his neighbour out of the house across the road, who joined in by dancing an impromptu jig.

He loves Dorset. 'What's not to like? We got it all ain't we? Got seaside, got moorland, got village and pub – whole damn lot is here.'

# Malcolm Cluett
## Dairy Farmer

Cluett is a French name, and Malcolm's ancestors came over with William the Conqueror. He has lived in a beautiful Dorset farmhouse, where the stones compete with the ivy, for 64 of his 66 years. Malcolm betrays my stereotype of a farmer in that he lives alone and has no dog, no cat, and no chickens pecking in the yard. But their absence allows more time for the 72 cows in his dairy herd, of whom he is obviously fond. Despite having numbers not names, Malcolm did admit to having favourites, usually identified by the amount he cusses them. Number 95, very evidently in calf, was particularly special with 62 coming a close second. He doesn't keep a bull, but a man with a rod sorts out that side of things when the time comes, he explained!

I assume he simply couldn't imagine living anywhere else, for it really was the most idyllic rural setting, with stunning far reaching views across the Blackmore Vale.

We had missed the hunt by a couple of hours when we visited his farm, but Malcolm doesn't have time for hunting and 'wouldn't be caught on an 'orse – too bloody dangerous!' Like so many other of the true Dorset characters we have met, Malcolm said it as it was. Refreshingly straightforward in his approach, he seemed to have his life organised just as he wanted it.

No farmer would be complete without his tractor. Malcolm rattled around in an ancient beast, well rusted and worn. When I asked him about the large dent at the front he explained it makes the cows go faster. 'They lie down till you drive at 'em then they get up and start eating.'

As we squelched through inches of mud, he warned us not to let the cows out. 'I'm not chasing the bloody things.' I got the impression that Malcolm would not want to run under any circumstance. 'Why walk when you can drive? Walking's for townies,' he announced.

# Philippa and Martin Clunes
## Television Producer and Actor/Farmer

It is tempting when you meet someone you've seen on your television screen, or read about in the papers, to assign traits, based on their public persona. Martin Clunes, much loved television personality, known for his comic roles and portrayal of wild men, in shows such as 'Doc Martin' and 'Men Behaving Badly' isn't like those characters in real life. In the safe haven of his idyllic home near Beaminster, high above sea level with views spanning miles, no noise but for the mooing of a lonely member of his livestock, he is rather steady, relaxed and charming.

He and his producer wife, Philippa, love Dorset – which they first made their home some sixteen years ago. 'We fell in love with it,' Martin told us. 'We had no plans to move or buy a second home or anything.'

Philippa added, 'We had a flat in the City of London right opposite the Globe and had this city life. Then we went to a wedding in Corfe Castle and thought, wow this is nice, maybe we'll just get a little weekend cottage. We half-heartedly started looking and it was an excuse to come to Dorset really. Neither of us knew it.'

Martin explained how they'd stay in hotels and go and see a few houses at weekends. 'I still remember standing at the top of Dorchester High Street and looking down that swoop.' It got more and more serious and eventually they employed a house hunter and thought, let's just do it.

Dorset also appealed as neither of them had a history here. Philippa told us, 'It wasn't like you are having to tap into someone's friends or old boy network which would be horrific. So it was kind of nice starting together. We wanted a little cottage and ended up with a huge vicarage in Powerstock, which was mad for weekends and we loved it. Then we had

a daughter and we had to decide London or Dorset. It became a no brainer and we decided to make the move. Our daughter is so country you just couldn't put her in London. She's Dorset born and bred pretty much, but we will always be incomers.'

The farm is home to sheep, cattle, 13 horses and an eclectic pack of dogs. Philippa grows all their own vegetables. 'We do get snowed in up here and we know we are going to be all right.'

Martin added, 'We are self-sufficient in haylage; we make enough for all the horses and all the beasts in the winter and we sell some.'

The Clunes do an amazing amount for Dorset and its charities, most notably by hosting the Buckham Fair for the last 5 years. 18,000 people attended in 2013, and there were over 800 dogs in the dog show. They felt it was a really good way of containing the requests from all the charities, so they don't feel so bad about saying no to the ones they can't support. Philippa is on the board of the Weldmar Hospicecare Trust and Martin is Patron of Julia's House. 'The county has such a pride in both those places and really cherishes them. If you talk to the people they all say how lucky they are to work there – they are just special people I guess,' Martin said.

I wondered if it was difficult for Philippa being married to someone as well known as Martin. 'Not really – that's just our life.'

Martin added, 'We are not famous up here, except for the sheep! We know this hillside and some of our best friends live just over there. We are so lucky, really lucky.'

Maybe it's the people of Dorset who are the lucky ones, that this generous couple have chosen to make the county their home.

# Jonathan Clunies-Ross

## Autistic and Downs Syndrome Carer, Constructionist

If you were to judge on first appearance, Jonathan Clunies-Ross could be described as an eccentric, an impression reinforced if you drove past his house. In reality we found an intelligent, gentle and well-educated man whose colourful home is a form of protest. I asked him if he would describe himself as an artist but he felt that would be a pretty pretentious description.

Over the years he has developed two distinct parts to his garden. The front is what he describes as 'visual pollution', a richly varied display of wooden peacock-like creatures, the house painted pink and embellished with spots and fish, a brightly-painted outbuilding with dancing figures, television monitors on the roof and a bisected bright green boat coming out of it. The driveway was once covered in plastic milk bottle tops, blue, red and a few purple, which crunched as satisfyingly as gravel as you walked across them. These are now being used as insulation in the respite home for the terminally ill on which he has now embarked.

By contrast, the back garden is natural and peaceful with a pond that attracts moorhens and kingfishers, and a willow bridge leading to a small island. It is somewhere you might wish to sit and reflect for a while, a haven of tranquillity. There are constructions dotted all round of various designs – mostly unfinished – as Jonathan once feared the planners would make him pull them down, but now he has now been granted permission and hopes to finish what he's

started.

Most of the materials have been pulled from skips. One construction has a particularly striking floor made from softwood logs, positioned end grain up, which will be polished to reveal their natural red colour. His intention was to create spaces where he could hold basket-weaving workshops and teach carving. He also wanted to create an environment where those looking after terminally ill people could come to recharge their batteries.

Moving back to the front of the house, there is a pink bath held aloft on a trailer at the front of the driveway and a stationary Volkswagen Beetle housing two Guy Fawkes-like figures. Jonathan's own car has frogs glued on to the bonnet to represent metamorphosis, along with the symbol for Om, the initial Sanskrit sound, a coil representing the spiritual or scientific big bang. There is quite a lot to take in!

When not working on his 'constructions', Jonathan is a carer for autistic adults at Ivers in Marnhull which offers care and support for those with learning disabilities, and he occasionally opens his home to various charities.

# Mark Constantine
## Co-founder of Lush

Dressed in an eye-catching Paul Smith jacket, Mark Constantine arrived to meet us on his bicycle as he doesn't drive. He is friendly and engaging. The new Lush offices, right on the sea front in Poole Harbour, are most definitely lush, something to smile about, and not like a working environment at all – with lots of space, plenty of wood, stunning views, and young people busy on laptops.

Mark was brought up in Weymouth and 'very nice it was too. It gives you a certain view on life. When I meet other Weymouth people they seem to have a similar sort of outlook, I don't know quite what it is.'

His was a sad childhood, due to his father leaving him and his mother. The absence of a father coloured Mark's early life, though he was fortunate to be brought up, 'by my mum, my nan and an aunt, who would come and go, and used to give me comics and sweets on Saturdays.'

In his late teens he went through a particularly difficult period, and one which a less strong personality might never have recovered from. He and his mother went to live with a stepfather, a disaster that ended up with Mark being thrown out and living in woods just outside Dorchester. 'I think it was probably two or three months when I was completely homeless. I didn't just live in the woods. I stayed with one person for a night, then I'd be in the woods for three nights – that kind of thing. I just couldn't afford a room though I was working every hour God sent me as an apprentice hairdresser.'

In the early 1970s, Mark, aged 18, made his way to London and got a job working for Elizabeth Arden in Bond Street. His aim was to become a theatrical make-up artist as in Weymouth he had done all the make-up for the amateur dramatic societies. But he lacked A level Art and an apprenticeship at the BBC was out of the question in those days for a boy.

Fortunately he was helped financially by the Gordon Boys Charitable Trust, of which he is now a trustee. 'I learned the power of charity from them – how small sums of money can make a dramatic difference. I can remember bursting into tears when they gave me a little extra for Christmas.'

After the IRA bombings when his wife Mo, whom he had met in Weymouth, arrived at work to find her office windows blown out, they decided to return to Dorset. In 1977 Mark set up Constantine & Weir, with beautician Liz Weir. From their small premises in Parkstone, Liz performed beauty treatments and Mark carried out hair and scalp consultations. All the products were concocted, using natural ingredients, by Mark and Mo in their kitchen.

Mo, who was assistant to the Clerk of the Courts in Poole, supported Mark whilst he got his fledgling business off the ground. 'I think Mo and the Charitable Trust saved me. She chose me and sorted me out and I've felt that all through my life – her influence, you know, building me up.'

Soon after starting in business, Mark heard about The Body Shop, got in touch, and dazzled Anita Roddick with his company's products. So began a long term relationship between the two companies which allowed Constantine & Weir to create new categories of bathing products.

Time marched on and, sensing a growing trend for mail order, they decided to launch Cosmetics to Go in 1988, striking out on their own whilst trying not to upset what had become an intense and flourishing business relationship with The Body Shop. So intertwined were the businesses that The Body Shop spent millions purchasing the formulae of the best sellers CTG made for them.

Mark was totally driven to make his business work, though there were hiccups along the way. In later life when he found his father again, sadly only six weeks before he died, he was able to tell him that maybe he was just trying to impress him with his hard work, commitment, and determination to succeed. 'It's called the entrepreneur's wound isn't it. Lots of businessmen have similar backgrounds.'

Many of the staff at Lush today were at Cosmetics to Go, which went into receivership in 1994. The next year, having learned from his mistakes, with renewed determination, Lush emerged, phoenix-like, the name having been selected in a competition, and retaining the original ethos of using minimal preservatives and not testing products on animals. Many of the iconic Lush products were dreamt up and invented at CTG and the Lush mission statement includes the sentence, 'We believe in long candlelit baths, sharing showers, massage, filling the world with perfume and in the right to make mistakes, lose everything and start again.'

His ultimate aim? Mark thought about his answer, saying he didn't want to sound trite. 'I think if you can you should,' he finally said. 'If you can you should, because there are so many people that can't for one reason or another, or feel they can't. I'm glad I got it out without it being too awful!'

Mark would also like to create a good stable business model but won't go much above a thousand shops in the next few years, hoping the internet side of the business, Lush Digital, will grow dramatically.

He touched briefly on his ongoing battle with Amazon, who are using the word 'lush' to describe bath and cosmetic products on their website. He has trademarked the name of an Amazon employee and produced a shower gel in his name, describing the product as 'rich, thick and full of it', though he says he will never market it, but was having a bit of fun (and maybe a touch of revenge) on someone he considers is behaving in an unreasonable way.

Hand in hand with Mark's success as a businessman is his love of ornithology. He has written a few books on bird watching – an activity he is intensely keen on – and thinks Poole Harbour almost the perfect place for it because of the sheer number of species found within its boundaries. His love and respect of the environment is well documented, and an awareness of

where products come from is central to the ethos of Lush. As an example, they are phasing out the use of palm oil, as palm trees form part of the habitat of the orangutan.

Reluctantly I closed our discussion with Mark telling me he'd never sued a journalist yet and had wanted to have some idea of my questions in advance to make sure interviews aren't just the same old bland routine. Had I known that I might have conducted things very differently, and who knows what else we might have discovered about this fascinating man with his rags to riches story, environmental conscience, passion for ornithology and mischievous approach to running one of the country's most successful businesses.

# Graeme Coombs
## Sparmaker

Regrettably Graeme Coombs died a short while after our meeting in 2012. However, we have included him as a 'Great Face' as we were both touched by the warmth of this wonderful and unforgettable character.

At his peak, Graeme could turn out 1500 thatching hazel or willow spars in a day. When we met him, aged 70, he was unwell and that impressive production rate had reduced, but illness had certainly not dampened his *joie de vivre*. The jolliest man you could meet with a big round, florid face – think Christmas pudding, and a tummy to match. He was dressed in country clothes with a suede looking waistcoat, sturdy boots and a huge, welcoming smile. He had rubber protectors on his knees as he worked deftly, whilst chatting and grinning. I asked him what they were called. He roared with laughter, as did his lovely wife

and daughter, Lisa. 'Knee knaps' he said. 'You just made that up!' said his wife!

Born in Shaftesbury, Graeme then moved to Margaret's Marsh. His father was a sparmaker, who taught Graeme when he was eight. 'As soon as you could use a hook you had to do it,' he told us. The young Graeme didn't get paid for his sparmaking but did manage to make some pocket money by catching and selling rabbits for 1/6d (7½p) each.

After leaving school, Graeme worked as a mechanic then moved to King's Stag when his father became licensee of The Green Man. He developed a passion for motorbike scrambling in the 1960s, 'them were the best days of my life'. His father continued making spars whilst running the pub but Graeme took over

from him in the 1970s, originally charging around £8 for 1000. 'Do you enjoy sparmaking?' I asked him.
'Must do I s'pose.'

Graeme was National Speed Sparmaking Champion in 1997 and 1998, and his personal record remains 107 spars in 15 minutes. He supplied spars internationally, including for the biggest single expanse of thatch in the world, which is in the US. He was proud of that and admitted to answering the phone 'Coombs in Europe' for a while. He obviously had lots of friends and the shelf in his shed was covered in decades of rings made by coffee cups, where his many visitors had stopped to chat. They, like us, must have found it hard to tear themselves away from this much-missed true Dorset character.

# Anthony 'Dick' Dalley
## Retired Swanherd

Anthony 'Dick' Dalley officially retired in 2001, after fifty years working at Abbotsbury Swannery. But over ten years later he is still often found there, leaning on his swanherd's crook, beautifully crafted in hazel with a ram's horn hook, which he uses for catching swans round the neck.

He was brought up at Chickerell, so doesn't consider himself a 'local' as it is nine miles up the road from Abbotsbury! When he was first offered the job at the Swannery he said, 'I'm not going out to

Abbotsbury, they're not civilised out there. But then I met my wife and we did eventually get here.'

Giving up his job in the fruit trade, Dick started a new life at the Swannery in 1961 as a swankeeper, living in an old cottage called Clouds Hill on the edge of the Fleet lagoon. It was very basic but did have electricity. Abbotsbury Swannery and its famous colony of mute swans, so called because of their lack of a loud call, has been part of the Ilchester Estates since the Dissolution of the Monasteries in 1539.

geese) who overwinter on the Fleet.

The Swannery is important, not only for the survival of this the only managed colony of nesting mute swans in the world, but also for scientific purposes, as an educational establishment and to give pleasure to the many visitors who come each year to admire these majestic birds. Lloyds of London use Abbotsbury quills to write in their records of shipping and other insurance losses, and the soft feathers under the wings of the swans are used decoratively on the helmets of the Queen's bodyguard, the Honourable Corps of Gentlemen at Arms.

Dick learned the hard way that swans can be dangerous. A single blow can be fatal. He was dealing once with a mother with cygnets when he was hit in the back of the neck by its mate, 'weighing 30 lbs going 30 mph, quite a weight to hit you when you're not expecting it.' The blow split open his head and knocked him out, but luckily Dick made a full recovery.

It would seem that Dick will never really retire. He is as much a part of Abbotsbury's famous Swannery as the swans themselves. I doubt he will ever move another nine miles from his home again either. 'Dorset's home. Somebody suggested going to Spain once, shan't do that again!'

Dick's responsibilities included fattening swans for Lord Ilchester's table, (eating them has since been banned). Later Dick was promoted to under-swanherd and eventually swanherd.

The earliest known record of the Swannery dates back to 1393 but it seems certain that a colony of mute swans had been nesting in the Fleet long before that time, attracted to its brackish but tidal waters as it is protected from the sea by Chesil Bank, an eight mile stretch of shingle. Each of the 600 or so swans consumes about eight pounds of plant food each day and the Fleet's shallow waters are rich in the eel grass on which they feed.

During winter food can become scarce. Corn is scattered in the water by the swanherds in early spring to supplement the swans' diet, as well as that of up to 20,000 other waterfowl (mostly wigeon and Brent

# Zara Dampney
## Athlete, Beach Volleyball

Behind Zara Dampney's enviable physique is a self-confessed 'girly girl' who's just as happy to talk about clothes and fashion as the competitive world of Beach Volleyball. She was utterly focused when she was in training and never seemed to question her commitment to the 2012 London Olympics, something which meant giving up three years full-time after she had completed a law degree.

Beach volleyball is played by two teams of two players on a sand court divided by a net. To keep the ball in play a team can only hit the ball up to three times before returning it over the net and try to ground it on the opponent's court. It has been an Olympic sport since the 1990s. Training is arduous and involved three weight, two cardio and ten sand sessions each week. Along with her Team GB partner, Shauna Mullin – Zara admits they were quite a 'feisty team' – she had some highs and lows and the girls and their coach developed a great way of reviewing their performance post match. They had a 'hot debrief' where they could let their emotions out, essential for girls, she says, and then the next day had a 'cold debrief' which was more strategic, productive, and sensible.

Zara has recently retired from the sport to help her parents run their home, Parley Manor, as a wedding venue. Despite hanging up the red bikini, she still maintains her fitness and healthy eating regime.

'It's quite hard when you are constantly competing. Although I am naturally quite competitive it's not a girl thing to be like that all the time. I used to find that quite tiring.'

# Mike Davies
## Cheesemaker

Dorset Blue Vinny cheese was reputedly Thomas Hardy's favourite. 'Vinney', as it is sometimes spelt, means mouldy in Dorset dialect, and although that might suggest it held some moisture it was originally considered a dry cheese. Production of Blue Vinny, which had been made for 300 years, ceased in the late 1950s due to a lack of demand.

Fortunately, Mike Davies, looking for a use for surplus milk in the 1980s, decided it was just the cheese he wanted to start making again. It wasn't easy, to get the process perfect, but now he produces a hundred 6 kilo, rich, blue cheeses each week – a journey to perfection that Mike reckons took seven years.

The making room is where you can find Mike for up to two hours each day. He grades the cheese with a special iron designed to extract a small portion of it, to check for blueness and maturity. It takes real skill to ensure the blue comes from the middle outwards ('vinney' is also thought to be a corruption of the word veiny). Temperature, hand pressing, wrapping, spiking to aerate the cheese, and turning are all carefully controlled. Nearly every process from the stirring of the unpasteurised milk in its huge heated bath with rennet and starter, to the packing of the cheeses ready for market, is done by hand.

Half of his limited production of Dorset Blue Vinny, made with skimmed cow's milk, is sold by specialist cheese shops in London. The rest goes all over the country to delicatessens, farm shops and restaurants as well as their strong local following and into the award-winning soups developed by his daughter Emily, which they also produce for the River Cottage label. Mike has rescued Blue Vinny from undeserved obscurity, winning many awards over the years, including three Great Taste Awards and the Taste of Dorset 'best cheese in Dorset' Award.

# Andrew Dike
## Dike & Son Ltd

The Dike family have been in Stalbridge since 1851 when their first small premises was opened. Today Dike & Son Ltd, now a superstore standing just behind the original site, boasts a wholesale and retail bakery, butchery, fish, delicatessen and hot food counters, licensed café, grocery and confectionery. They stock over 100 local products which come from within a twenty mile radius and suppliers approach them all the time with new mouth-watering products.

It is still run as a family business with Andy Dike as Managing Director and his mother Deidre as Company Secretary. Andy has one brother who is not involved in the family firm but coaches sport, including cricket, which is also Andy's passion and he plays for the Stalbridge XI as often as time allows.

Their father, William, was also a cricketer, as well as a car enthusiast, and their vintage delivery vehicles, some of which are shown in the photograph on this page, are very special. The collection includes a 1917 Model T Ford, named 'Georgina' after Andy's eldest daughter, which was the first motorised vehicle they had and took over the deliveries previously carried out by horse and cart. 'She's a beauty this one; really fond of her.'

They also own a 1951 Ford, called 'Emily' by Andy's father, starting the tradition of naming the vehicles, which is driven round by Father Christmas in December, and a more modern Morris Minor, 'Belinda', named after Andy's second daughter. The cars have appeared at various vintage rallies and steam fairs, including The Great Dorset Steam Fair, and are maintained by an enthusiast.

As well as the vintage motor cars, Andy's father, William, also had a dream. He wanted to create a superstore on their site in Stalbridge. Market research indicated that anything larger than 8,000 feet would be over ambitious. But so convinced was William

that their superstore would be a success that he went ahead with building a 22,000 square feet premises. Tragically, William died before the project was completed but he did live to see the foundations being dug.

His optimism has been borne out by events, for the business is thriving and has a wonderfully vibrant atmosphere. As William would have wanted, it is very much the social hub of Stalbridge and the surrounding area, with people chatting in the aisles or stopping for coffee in the café. The staff are encouraged to talk to the customers as much as they want – no rushing them through the checkout.

Dike's has won many awards since the new store opened in 2007, including Best Independent Food Shop three times and South West Champion for Local Food in the Countryside Alliance Awards.

Andy likes to be as hands on as possible, rolling his sleeves up and getting to work on the shop floor in Stalbridge and also at their small outlet in Crewkerne. Andy respected his father's decision that he must prove himself in the industry so he trained with Misselbrook and Weston, now part of Tesco, for three years before he felt ready to join the family firm. He

also had a year in Australia and New Zealand which he told us 'opened his eyes to the big wide world.'

In July this year Dike's supermarket went online, though Andy would much rather see his customers in the store. Some of them have known him since he was a small boy and he feels great affection for them. He recognises, however, that many prefer the convenience of internet shopping. They already deliver locally, mainly to the elderly, who fax or telephone their orders and this will continue.

Andy's goal is to make visitors to his shop feel welcome and this, along with stocking good local produce, has been their focus since 1851. He can remember his great uncle Cyril, 'a real people person', introducing newcomers to the villagers. Andy's dream is to be able to pass his family business onto the next generation. If one of his daughters, or his son, William, now three years old, do take over they will be the sixth generation to run this friendly establishment, which has now served the local community for over 160 years.

# Rebecca Dixon
## Teacher

Ten years ago Rebecca was a young actress 'between jobs' and looking for some work that would fit in with bringing up small children. Her father, a carpenter at Guys Marsh Prison, suggested she apply for a teaching post there. Rebecca got the job and worked for her postgraduate certificate in education whilst teaching literacy to the inmates.

Rebecca ran eight week 'roll on roll off' courses as prisoners tend to move through the system. She was not daunted by entering the tough world of an all male category C prison, which holds a complete mix of non high security prisoners. Once inside, however, it is only the fencing and barbed wire that distinguish it from any other educational establishment.

Relaxed and gentle, she made a stark contrast to her students. Her patience and understanding so instilled confidence they agreed to us attending a session to watch their progress. The respect they showed Rebecca was remarkable. Her honest easy manner and genuine desire to help made those attending her literacy class take trouble to read each word correctly, demonstrating real pride in each small but significant achievement.

'I hope I am making a difference but unfortunately reoffending rates are shockingly high. I give them all the positive information I can, but sometimes they just don't have the skills to survive outside prison.'

It could take time to persuade students that learning to read and write were essential, with cries of 'Miss, Miss, I don't want to be here. This isn't for me.' Within a few weeks such complaints usually changed to, 'If I thought it was this easy I'd have done it earlier.'

With valuable experience gained, Rebecca has recently left teaching at Guys Marsh because she was finding it difficult working during school holidays. She is now a learning support teacher at St Mary's,

Shaftesbury, helping 11 to 18 year old girls with their studies; quite a contrast, but one that requires no less patience and kindness. She has not ruled out a return to teaching at a prison, and is certain education is absolutely fundamental to helping people change their lives for the better.

# Clive Farrell
## Entomologist

We watched, captivated, as we stood with Clive Farrell in his butterfly house. He licked his finger for moisture to try and attract a butterfly resting on the tropical leaf next to him. He was hoping to lure the elusive blue morpho butterfly to sit on his head for a photograph, but he had nearly a hundred other beautiful creatures, of many species, to choose from, which fluttered coquettishly around us. This was a special moment, simply standing there, enjoying the warmth of the greenhouse, the beauty of the insects and the enthusiasm of their keeper.

Initial descriptions of Clive, prior to our meeting him, conjured up an eccentric; someone living in a Michael Jackson-esque fantasy insect world. In reality, Clive is much more than those things. He is considered, extremely knowledgeable and enjoys the reaction of gasping admiration he inevitably gets from people when they enter his hundred acre estate, with its plant prison (where the prickly and unruly botanical species are kept), bramblearium (housing 77 different brambles), spiral garden, snake house, butterfly greenhouses and much more.

Clive originally trained as a solicitor, became wealthy through property, and was able to buy Ryewater Nursery, near Sherborne, to indulge his love of butterflies. His lepidopteran empire extends to Florida, as well as Belize, Stratford-upon-Avon and Syon Park in London – where he built his first butterfly house. He entered into a massive project in St Albans a few years ago, intended as the biggest butterfly attraction in the world, but 'my heart ruled my head and things spiraled out of control and I had to withdraw. It is still going, but it is a forlorn thing to see. Lots of visitors come to see the gardens but it isn't finished.'

As we strolled round with Clive it became apparent that his imagination knows no bounds. Luckily he has a garden designer, Ivan Hicks, who shares his creativity and is able to put these ideas into a reality in the form of plant beds, structures, gates, and landscaping. You really have to visit to understand the bizarre nature of the enterprise and the wonderful freedom at play there.

As we left the more manicured gardens and went into the wilder bramblearium, Clive was in his element. The only green butterfly, the rare green hairstreak, landed nearby and Clive rushed toward it with childlike fascination at the sighting of this delicate insect. We then saw a small blue which pleased him even more. 'It's living here, with me,' he proclaimed with a beaming smile, as we neared a patch of its only plant food, kidney vetch. Clive told us 'there are around 60 British species of butterfly including migrants, and you can probably find 55 of them in Dorset, so it is probably the richest county for butterfly species.'

Clive's eyes twinkled as he told us about the gnome we were looking for as we continued our walk. 'On a sunny day he is usually on his window seat. He makes blackberry wine so this is his orchard here and you can see all his bottles inside his house. He is 230 years old and has a peg leg, as sadly he lost one in a fishing accident. He is based on a book called *The Little Grey Men* by BB, about the last gnomes in England, and is waiting for his brothers to join him.'

So magical was our visit that we really wanted to believe him, and you can imagine that for the children who visit Ryewater Nursery there is no question that they are in a wonderland. I doubt they realise how lucky they are that Clive is prepared to share it with them.

# Lord and Lady Fellowes of West Stafford
## Writer, Actor, Director and Charity President

We found Julian Fellowes at his desk on a Sunday morning working on the script for the fourth series of 'Downton Abbey'. It was really quite surreal to think that what he was creating will absorb up to a third of the adult population of this country for nearly an hour every Sunday evening from September. It was incredibly tempting to take a peek, or to bring Sybil back to life and kill off the loathsome O'Brien, with a few taps of the keyboard.

Julian's wife Emma is not allowed near his computer as she has 'magnetic fingers and would probably ruin something'. She does, however, have a computer of her own from which she runs an incredibly hectic life; chairing and supporting countless charities, notably the Lord Kitchener National Memorial Fund, an educational charity of which she is President; reading through all Julian's scripts, which she does in bed in her locked bedroom with no telephones and no dogs; organising the extensive renovations to their beautiful house, and no doubt coordinating a whirl of social events both in Dorset and London.

Emma says, 'You do sometimes feel like an octopus and every single one of your legs is being pulled.' However she is self-effacing enough to admit that if you don't have that (the hard work) you don't have the other (presumably the perks). Their daily post can contain up to fifty requests: can you read this? can you do this? can you help me get a part? will you see my cousin?' According to Julian 'you just feel flattened'.

Despite so busy a life they both appear calm, relaxed and utterly charming. Emma is exceptionally striking and elegant in her stylish clothes and trademark turban. She says she wears one practically every day, unless she is wearing a tiara! We wandered round their gardens with their dogs, and they willingly posed for the photographs. They made no fuss about standing in the River Frome in pouring rain, and Emma sat patiently in her immaculate and cosy fisherman's hut. This sanctuary houses games for visiting children, coal for the stove, Smarties for the peckish and paper and pen for the creative. A more idyllic setting you could not find and the whole scene was not unlike the atmosphere of 'Gosford Park', for which Julian won the Oscar for Best Original Screenplay, or 'Downton Abbey', winner of countless awards.

Julian has also written two successful books, written and directed several other successful films and series, and is himself an accomplished actor. He is thus well placed to take a view on people who might be considering a career in acting and knows only too well that the odds against succeeding are extremely high. 'If you are not gorgeous I'd advise you to give it a miss!' Something Emma was rather upset by as she doesn't believe that looks should count, but, as Julian explained, he was merely stating a fact.

Julian's reason for his success are simple. 'My gift, if I have one, is understanding why people do what they do and that interests me. The extent that people are blind to their own motives and choices. I am always fascinated by that. Most people have a sort of key virtue that they think trumps the others.'

Lord and Lady Fellowes came to Dorset over a decade ago. Emma grew up in Hampshire, Julian in Sussex and neither of them wanted to be in their childhood counties. They both wanted to be near the sea, in a house with a decent library. They wanted running water in the garden and ended up with three rivers.

Julian's grandmother once told him, 'Always remember when you move to the country, dear, that people who are easy to meet are difficult to get rid of!' To which Emma had the final word. 'But we haven't wanted to shake anyone off in Dorset because they are all so gorgeous.'

# Alice Fox-Pitt
## Broadcaster

Alice Plunkett, as she is known in the racing world, is one of those rare people who genuinely doesn't seem to notice how outstanding she is. In her own words, 'I somehow ended up being the only girl to have ridden round the Grand National course, in the Fox Hunters' Chase, and Badminton.' It was this, combined with her relaxed style and impressive knowledge, that led to her becoming a household name in television broadcasting.

'I was riding at the Cheltenham Festival, and they had something called Festival Radio there. The guy producing it asked me if I could get people out of the weighing room for interviews. We got on really well so the next year he gave me my own show. They called it 'Waking up with Alice'. Then someone from Epsom and Royal Ascot heard it and asked me to do the same for the Derby and Ascot, and so I did that. Someone from Sky asked me to do a screen test and I got a job for the Racing Channel, as it was then.' Alice was still eventing, sponsored by Racing Green, so the radio and television work was then just a side-line.

In 2000, however, she thought it would be a good time to stop riding professionally. Although long-listed for the Sydney Olympics, she didn't feel she was going to get on the 2004 team, and her horses were getting old. Fortuitously she landed a fantastic job doing a series on the 12 million dollar races round the world so, aged only 27, she was doing hour long live shows from Australia, Dubai and Hong Kong.

The timing was perfect. 'It was good to get away because it is a very difficult thing to stop a sport. It's addictive and you always think next year is going to be your year. There are so many girls who just live the dream, but are never going to be good enough and actually being involved with William showed me that. He is on a different stratosphere to what I was.'

Alice's laid back approach might lead you to believe she is rather scatty (she told of us of losing a shoe in the mud on a live show but having to hop on, regardless!). She is however, totally switched on and well informed. Impressively, whilst we chatted, she nursed a new born baby (she also has two sons), made the coffee and dealt with telephone calls – a masterclass in multi-tasking!

# William Fox-Pitt
## Equestrian and Event Rider

There is an abundance of information about William Fox-Pitt available, but what none of it describes is his modesty. He is certainly cool and considered, but gave no sense of having to shout about his achievements. You can only begin to imagine the forest of rosettes bursting out of the walls in his yard. William has so many titles and Olympic medals to his name that I will not attempt to list them all, but he is

absolutely expert in his field, having been Eventing's World number 1 three times (the first British rider to hold the title) and British number 1 eleven times. He has recently won his third Rolex Kentucky, this time on 'Bay My Hero'. Quite simply, he is one of the most successful British event riders of all time.

William is striking and exceptionally tall, and anyone with only a passing interest in horses could be forgiven for asking whether he isn't too tall to be a rider. He is amazingly hard working, spending up to eight hours a day in the saddle. William never has a day off; he works the horses every day, whatever the weather. The eight people who work for him at his eventing stables near Sturminster Newton are all busy and in tune, but relaxed; the whole operation appears slick and productive.

I asked him what was the secret to his success. 'His wife!' chirped Alice. William's reply was more considered, saying it was 'mostly down to circumstances and having the right horse, at the right time, at the right event.' Alice also added that single-mindedness and dedication were key.

They make a great team. With her technical expertise and their shared love of horses, Alice can offer tips whilst watching William ride and you know what they say, behind every great man . . .

William's favourite horse is 'Gaucho', though the photograph on the previous page shows him on 'Tops', whom he loves as he is very relaxed. William prefers a lazier horse as you know where you stand with them. A faster, livelier one can be unpredictable.

Despite his extraordinary success William doesn't appear to be complacent about any of it and is grateful to his numerous, big name, sponsors, such as Jeep and Musto, whose support and funding allow him to get on with what he does best.

His middle names, Speed and Lane, caused some amusement when he was stopped aged 17, for driving too fast. On another occasion, though William stresses it was a couple of decades later, the local constabulary had cause to give him a ticket again and took the opportunity to ask for an autograph at the same time.

William is also a keen (and probably very good) skier but didn't take to the slopes prior to the 2012 Olympics. 'There are some risks you have to take and some you don't.'

William is also a huge fan of chickens and his wife Alice jokingly said that, 'if he gave up the horses that's what he do – poultry farming.'

# Hayley Foy
## Farrier

As a young girl at primary school, Hayley was petrified of horses. When her bicycle had a puncture her older sister persuaded her to ride her pony. She was then forced to continue when her father threatened to sell it. Finally she was won over. Now her working life revolves round horses and she is out, in all weathers, filing hooves, firing and moulding shoes and fitting them to her, not always compliant, equine clients. On a busy day she will fit around five to eight sets, re-using shoes where possible and always with a cheery smile.

Eight years ago, after qualifying at a training college for farriers, Hayley set up in business on her own. She had been saving up to buy the necessary equipment and, with some help from her father, was able to get together a van, a stock of shoes, forge and other tools – all costing around £5,000. Since then she has never looked back or needed to advertise. Many of her customers are surprised to meet a female farrier as it is a physically demanding job, bent double for up to eight hours a day and dealing with powerful horses who might be frightened or alarmed at her presence. Hayley has perfected a good technique however and getting the horse to do the work for her is key. 'It shouldn't be a wrestling match! I like the remedial side of it all – doing work with feet out of balance, mending problems, making lame horses sound. I enjoy doing that. It's good.'

She is the show farrier for the Aldon Horse Trials each year and has shoed horses for Mary King and William Fox-Pitt. She really can't imagine doing anything else and says her job is a lifestyle choice, not something someone should go into half-heartedly. 'I'm Hayley Foy the Farrier,' she says. 'My job is part of who I am.'

# Jo Freestone
## Burlesque Dancer

In a dingy upstairs room in Sherborne, late on a Thursday night, Jo Freestone, burlesque dancer and founder of Barmy Burlesque and BAPS (Burlesque Academy for Performing Showgirls) is putting five girls through their paces, rehearsing a routine for an upcoming show. Shreds of feather boa are strewn all over the floor, as are long satin gloves, the odd high heeled shoe and garter. 'Showgirl smiles,' instructs Jo, and the girls, laced into corsets, strutting deftly on huge platform and high sparkly shoes, fake eyelashes a flutter, respond.

'That's it darling. You need to learn to change quickly, strip slowly. And again . . . from the top.'

Jo is encouraging to her students and was inspired to set the business up in 2009 to 'make women feel fabulous' as well as a way of keeping fit. Her background is in musical theatre and drama and this comes across in the surprisingly professional way she takes the class, whilst 'keeping it all in the best possible taste!'

She has created a persona as Major Outrage, putting on shows for private parties. Her students, some with names chosen to continue the military theme, Private Parts, General Strike and Corporal Punishment, clearly enjoy their classes and describe the amazing bond between them all. They often get together to make tassles, fans and decorate their bras and costumes for shows. Many have forged close friendships, and two of the girls travel all the way from Weymouth for Jo's classes.

She doesn't advocate sitting on customers' laps. 'I did that once, sat on a chap's knee and his leg fell off. It must have been the way I wriggled!' Jo is no shrinking violet. She described a journey she took on the London underground dressed as Major Outrage on her way to a performance. A fellow passenger asked her what she did with her whip. 'What do you think I do?' replied Jo, and ordered him to stand up and bend over, whereupon she whipped him.

We discussed the pleasures of living in the Dorset

countryside. Do you go for lovely walks, I asked, 'No!' Jo replied emphatically. She is, however, thinking of a collaboration with the Morris dancers, so I wouldn't rule out seeing her striding across the open fields, whip in hand and suspenders on, sometime soon.

# Stephen Fudge
## Biscuit Baker

Founded by Steve's great uncle nearly 100 years ago, Thomas J Fudge's Remarkable Bakery has plenty to shout about. With sublime new packaging, redesigned products and new lines added, their 100 or so biscuit varieties, sweet and savoury, continue to delight the people of Dorset and beyond.

Steve didn't intend to go into the family business, but after a spell as an apprentice confectioner in Germany, he came back to join his brother Graham and sister-in-law, Sue, in the family firm in 1989. It was a good decision and the bakery near Stalbridge today produces mouth-watering biscuits by the

hundreds of thousand each week – some lines almost completely by machine, others handmade or hand-dipped. Cheddar wafers and Florentines are by far the most popular, and, as well as their own brands, they bake for the Royal Household, Highgrove, Fortnum and Mason and M & S.

Steve's contribution is on the technical side; machinery, recipe development, logistics. Fortnum and Mason give them free shelf space where they test new concepts and they employ professionals to help them understand what consumers want. Steve explained, 'You don't buy our biscuits merely because you are hungry.' Though he did go on to say, 'I've been known to go into Waitrose, buy a packet of Cheddar wafers, go to a pub, buy a pint and eat the lot. Whenever we're at home and have friends round we hand round the product, but all you are looking at is people's faces. You don't actually appreciate what you're eating. You are just seeing their reaction.'

Steve is fond of Cerne Abbas, especially for the 'Layby Picnic Parties' he started there with friends over 30 years ago. They were so amazed that people stopped to eat at the side of the road, when they could be enjoying a beautiful rural view just round a corner, that they used to dress up in their dinner jackets and party frocks and enjoy grand picnics in the layby with a view of the Cerne Giant. Though Steve hasn't been for years, these extravagant picnics still take place annually in September.

Steve has more serious matters to attend to now. It is not how it was in his grandfather's day with everything staying the same: 'It was a penny a loaf for years. Now things can change overnight. The whole picture of retail is pretty well immediate.' If that means more buttery pufferies, moorish melts and scrumptious shards for us lucky consumers, I am not complaining!

# Dr Jane Goodall DBE

## Ethologist, Environmentalist, Conservationist and Primatologist

Dr Jane Goodall was born in Bournemouth when it was in Hampshire, and still spends time in her childhood home on the rare days she is not travelling the globe spreading the word on her world. She has had a rose and orchid named after her, is a United Nations Messenger of Peace and is globally recognised as *the* expert on chimpanzees.

She has also set up the Jane Goodall Institute, which includes a youth-led community action and learning programme, Roots and Shoots. It now operates in 132 countries, helping young people map their community to identify specific challenges and develop a plan for a solution.

Jane is obviously an animal lover and from our meeting it became apparent that she has a special relationship with Charlie, the dog in the photograph. Maybe it was the influence of Jane's presence, her peaceful demeanour that makes her feel she carries the calm of the forest within her, that allowed Charlie to be as much a part of the interview as Jane herself. Making noises that sounded almost human, Charlie, sat on laps, nuzzled the camera and generally interfered until she was the centre of attention.

Mr H, the stuffed toy monkey in the photograph (named after Gary Haun, the inspirational blind

magician) goes everywhere with Jane and has been stroked by millions in most countries on the planet, including North Korea. 'If I forget him there is a commotion. He's a mascot, yes, a symbol of the indomitable human spirit that is going beyond the mascot in a way.' Jubilee, the other stuffed toy close to Jane's heart, was given to Jane when she was 18 months old. It was about to travel to Germany with her to be given a close fitting fur coat, as his old one was badly worn. 'I don't like him like this, he's too naked, too sad.'

One thing we learned from Jane was the incredible bond she enjoyed with her equally remarkable mother. 'My mother was wise, brought my sister and I up in a very wise way; she was ahead of her time. When I said I love animals and she found earthworms in my bed, she said they need earth and we took them out together. Once I disappeared for over four hours trying to find out how a hen laid an egg; nobody knew I was hiding in the hen house. Instead of getting mad at me she sat down and told me the wonderful story of how a hen lays an egg.

'When I dreamed of going to Africa, aged 10, because I'd read Tarzan from cover to cover up my beech tree in the garden, and fallen in love with him and was furious that he had married the wrong Jane, I decided I would go to Africa and live with animals and write books about them. It was my mother who said, "Well if you really want something you work hard and never give up, you find a way."'

This was 1944 and Africa; girls absolutely didn't do that sort of thing. Jane did get to Africa, however. In 1956 she visited some friends in Kenya and, determined to return, worked as a waitress to get enough money together, going back in 1957. She met the anthropologist, Louis Leakey, who realised Jane was the person he had been looking for for ten years to help him study chimpanzees. He appointed her his secretary and she studied chimpanzees in various sites for the next four decades. Through patience and perserverance she was accepted by the primates and learned that they hunted for meat and used tools, activities previously assumed confined to humans. She also witnessed a darker side to chimpanzees and aggression which went as far as cannibalism.

During that time and encouraged by Leakey, she studied for, and achieved, a PhD in Ethology at Cambridge University, despite having no previous formal training.

Jane had only been given permission to go to Africa on the condition she took a companion, so her mother volunteered to accompany her. 'My father had gone off fighting in the war and then they divorced when I was twelve. I inherited his constitution because he never needed to eat and he could go all day without much food. He was a bit adventurous himself.

'I had malaria forty times altogether. You learn to live with it. You build up a certain resistance. Mum and I both nearly died in 1960, but we didn't. The doctor had told us there was no malaria, for some odd reason, so there was no prophylactic or anything.

'I didn't mind spiders but poor Mum didn't like them. We had this old fashioned ex-army tent. Today you have nice neat zipped ground sheets and mosquito net windows. We did have some thick netting over the window but the ground sheet was just a piece of

canvas and if you wanted air to come in you rolled up the side flaps and tied them with tape and so, yes, the air came in but so did snakes and spiders and centipedes. People say I was brave, no – my poor mother was though.'

We could have talked to Jane Goodall for hours but her time is precious and there isn't room here to describe much of her extraordinary life. Despite all the people she has met and influenced, and all the good she has done, she stills feels an affinity for Dorset. 'I love the beach and the cliffs in Dorset, that's where we go. Durley Chine and up and down Alum Chine and Middle Chine.' No doubt Charlie is leading the way and Jane, smiling her serene smile, happy just to follow.

# Adrian Gray
## Stone Balancing Artist

'I want to give a sense of wonder and for people to think "that's beautiful" or "that's magic."'

It's May, the weather has been appalling, with torrential, incessant rain. As a result we have had to cancel our appointment with Adrian Gray on more than one occasion, but finally we see a window of opportunity and dash to Lyme Regis. Hurrah, the sun comes out! We walk past the huts and holiday homes, shut up and forgotten despite the season, and carefully pick our way down the pebbly beach, and there we

find Adrian doing what Adrian Gray does. He is balancing impossibly large stones on top of other impossibly large stones in an asymmetric arrangement that doesn't seem feasible, not helped by the added challenge of a windy beach.

Adrian is a likeable and curious creature. Small in stature, but with a look of Indiana Jones about him, he is an artist first and foremost. His work is not so

much about balance but aesthetics. Although he does try and find the smallest point of contact between stones, to produce work that appears to defy gravity, what is most important to him is that the finished piece is a thing of beauty.

He works fairly quickly; selecting the right stones to start with is key. They can weigh from 10 to 100 kilos; it's just as well he's strong. He then 'listens with his fingers' until the centre of gravity is found and produces stunning pieces of art with these beautiful smooth or rough, dark or light, weather and sea-beaten rocks balanced in a stunning arrangement. No wonder he is often asked if he is using glue, or even if it is magic.

It is the meditative aspect of stone balancing that first attracted Adrian. He worked on adventure holidays in the Himalayas for many years, setting up his own company and helping people to achieve firsts; the first to climb a particular peak, first to swim from source to sea, first to swim across a crater lake. His clients loved the kudos of these achievements and Adrian clearly loved giving them the adventure. He became ill however, which led to post viral syndrome, and in 2000 came to live by the sea in Lyme Regis. Although he had worked a little with rocks, lining the pathways in the Himalayas with stone towers, he relished the peace and patience of trying to balance large stones on the beach in Dorset, a form of meditation which became part of his healing as well as his livelihood.

Now he photographs the results and sells prints and postcards. He also sells finished pieces that have been secured with a steel rod, but not without filming the balancing of them first, to prove that the stones can rest in that position with no stabilising steel. When we met him, he was preparing for a trip to Singapore where his work is being shown in a gallery there,

something he is obviously excited about. He has done television commercials and corporate promotional work where balancing of any type is key.

Adrian always get a fantastic reaction from people on the beach. 'I want to give a sense of wonder and for people to think "that's beautiful" or "that's magic."' He has learned a few tricks along the way; to face stones into the wind so they stay up better, tilting the base so there is not such an acute angle, and, selecting stones with a lovely curve or waist.

He seems to live in an ever evolving landscape at Lyme and although he does come across stones he has worked with before, and collects ones he particularly loves, the possibilities are endless. 'Every time you have a storm it's like a whole new palette of materials to work with.' So next time the weather is lousy and we grumble we can't get out to the beach, I shall think of how bad weather merely throws up new creative opportunities for Adrian and for us to marvel at.

# Daz Hallett
## Bodybuilder and Mr Universe

When people ask Daz Hallett's wife what he does and then learn he is a bodybuilder some pass comments such as 'Ooh I wouldn't like to meet him in a dark alley!' and conjure up an image of a great hulk, with an attitude to match. Daz doesn't fit this stereotype at all; bulky, yes, aggressive, no. It was his diminutive size that first led him to bodybuilding via the martial arts, and seems to me an act of self-discipline and self-esteem, not an exercise in 'look at me or don't mess with me!'

Originally from Stalbridge, Daz opened Fitness World in Weymouth a few years ago and trains there with plenty of regulars in a relaxed atmosphere. It was his wife who encouraged him to enter his first bodybuilding competition in Taunton in 2002 which he won. In 2012 he became the IBFA World Champion winning both his class (173 cm and under) and overall (approximately 280 competitors). In 2013 he won the IBFA Universe Italy, 1st Athletics class. To achieve this crown of Mr Universe Daz had to undergo a rigorous schedule of working out up to five times a day, eating only turkey and beans, to get his body fat down to 3%, and ensuring he was dehydrated enough to display his well-defined muscles. It's all about peaking on the day and Daz's knowledge of how his body works is the key to his success. On top of the physical conditioning we mustn't forget shaving and waxing off all his body hair, and applying up to four coats of tan to achieve a good dark sheen.

Daz loves Dorset for its proximity to the beach but claims not to notice admiring glances when he's there. An honest, gentle and dedicated man, we wish him well. He seems to stick to his own mantra of 'set your goals, aim for them and don't let anything else get in the way.'

# Treleven Haysom
## Retired Mason and Quarryman

There was a marked drop in temperature as we stepped down the huge chunks of stone, laid to enable an easy descent into the disused Purbeck stone quarry. By the light of Treleven Haysom's torch we could clearly see the definite layers of rock and the man-made tunnel through which the great blocks of Purbeck stone would have been dragged using horse power. Mechanisation has made today's industry a great deal less arduous but it was wonderful to see these clean, underground caverns where previous generations had toiled.

Trev, as he is known, is fascinated by, and extremely knowledgable about his work. Now retired, his son Mark runs the company, Haysom Purbeck Stone Ltd. Trev's family have quarried for generations, since 1698, in fact, when his ancestor Robert Haysom quarried the cliffs at Durlston Bay. Trev has got more than one quarry concession. There is the quarry at St Aldhelm's Head, the old Landers (now Haysom's) quarry at Langton Matravers, as well as one on the National Trust Estate and one on his own land in Swanage.

Trev learned his trade from his father. As a boy of about ten, he remembers his father working on the capitals for the Temple Church in London, built as their headquarters by the Knights Templar. He carved them all, which was a big achievement and something of which Trev is justifiably proud. 'My father was very skillful and very fast. He was a consummate letter cutter too.' Trev has enjoyed every aspect of his life as a stone mason and quarryman and started work as soon as he could: 'happiest day of my life when I left school!'

He has travelled to Newfoundland researching 18th century stone and toured graveyards there. He discovered a species of heather that grows over there which is exotic to North America and native to our Dorset heaths. 'I suggest that they were packing the stone in heather, readily available round Poole Harbour, to ensure its safety during transportation. Like bubble wrap.'

Generally quarrymen did not own land, paying a royalty on excavated stone to the landowner. In Purbeck the quarrymen also worked the stone, which was unusual.

Trev explained, 'In those days quarries had a natural limit because they were working underground. They also had a 100 foot rule. If word got round in the pub that good stone was coming out of a particular field you couldn't just go in and start digging right beside an existing quarry; you had to do it 100 feet away.'

Historically Purbeck quarrymen would have been making mostly paving stones. 'There are layers of stone coming out the ground about a paving thickness. All you do is square them up smooth them out and bingo. In 1800 there were almost a hundred quarries in Swanage employing hundreds of men all churning out paving, now there are only around seven quarries in Purbeck.'

Trev showed us dinosaur casts stuck on the wall of their museum which the old quarrymen called 'boils', not knowing what they were. We saw a huge bulge made by the infilling of an imprint of a diplodocus foot, the one from its next stride having probably never been found as it would be some distance away. Trev also showed us many prints made by three-toed dinosaurs making their way across the squashy surface millions of years ago. Finally he led us to a beautiful slab of stone awaiting its fate as a polished table top. A large ammonite fossil graced its surface. 'Imagine,' said Trev 'all across the Atlantic this sort of thing is happening to Coca Cola cans. Chuck a few million years at them and see what happens!'

# Minna Hepburn
## Fashion Designer

Minna seems to have the pace of her life just the way she wants it. Her two young children are at school, she goes to her London studio rarely, she rides her horse in the stunning Dorset countryside, her Canadian husband helps out with the children when she needs to travel, and her work involves creating delicate, alternative bridal wear, womenswear and childrenswear.

Minna is Finnish and has lived in Dorset for the last ten years. She started her business in 2008 with just a few tops which she made from material and garments found at vintage antique markets. She discovered a lace made in Scotland so tracked down the supplier, and that's where everything started. ' I've always loved vintage and old pieces but I never studied fashion. The old pieces have a story to tell.'

Minna does all her own PR, marketing and sales – relying heavily on social media such as Facebook and Twitter. It isn't easy promoting a fashion business. Minna explains, 'You might be in *Vogue* magazine and yet get no hits from it.'

The collection consists of around a hundred bride's dresses for customers to chose from and these can be altered to suit. Minna's creations are floaty, individual, not overly fitted and made with delicate lace, vintage fabrics, silk, beads, the odd feather. She has a strong customer base in Australia, but is not at the mercy of the latest trend. 'When you are a small label you cannot compete. I did try and I listened to the buyers, but there are no guarantees. Even if you get an order, they are tiny and then you get paid six months later for all that risk. I've been there and I thought this is not a nice business model, I don't want to be part of it.'

Minna feels strongly about the environmental issues and uses organic, recycled and locally produced textiles. Her label could be described as Eco Luxe and with a new children's collection recently added and a shop in Shaftesbury the brand is growing.

'Always when I start a collection I think about the beautiful meadow here in Dorset and I just picture a girl, barefoot, running around in a white dress. Nothing to do with a wedding, just something that always starts the creative process.

'Dorset is so much prettier than Finland. In Finland there is just one colour of green whereas here, in the summer there are different shades of green. It is just beautiful. People are quite narrow minded in Scandinavia but here in Dorset they talk to each other.'

# Lal Hitchcock
## Beachcomber and Environmental Artist

When I find rubbish on a Dorset beach, I virtuously carry it, dangling, to the nearest bin. Lal Hitchcock takes a much more positive and open attitude to debris on her beachcombing expeditions. She gathers what she thinks interesting, takes it home, washes it, categorises it and then creates something from it.

She has been known to sculpt objects on the beach and has done projects for Bridport Arts Centre that meant working in this way, but mostly the creating happens back at home. Lal explains 'The lovely thing about making is that I am in my own little world. I go back to that child place where I am completely absorbed. When it is working I can see where it is going and time has gone really quickly. My disbelief is suspended and I've got these little characters, and you are in the moment. It is a lovely place to be and I feel

for people who don't have that.'

Lal is happiest in Dorset. 'It is the environment that I live and work in and that my friends are in, so in a way I can't think of it as Dorset, I just think of it as home. If I was to move I wouldn't move very far away. There is a hillfort without a name on the Mapperton estate, Burcombe, I think. I go and sit up there on a spring evening with a friend and listen to the birds and watch the sun going down. Having walked up there, we come back in the dark and in midsummer, when the glow worms are out, see them glowing. Being on high ground gives you an overview so you can put things in context much more, so the little things that have been getting us down can be put down there.'

Likewise Lal enjoys the calming effect of the sea and its ability to energise, 'like breathing, the in and out and in and out.'

# Mark Hix
## Chef, Restaurateur and Food Writer

Our meeting with Mark Hix began at Hix Oyster and Fish house in Lyme Regis but within minutes we were hurrying down to the beach where the name was being painted on his boat. We then set off at a brisk pace so that Mark could fish for sea bass further along the coast. He was completely occupied with what he was doing and apart from the odd interruption on his mobile phone was very much focused on fishing. He was so busy, I began to wonder if we would ever have a chance to talk.

Foraging was next. First he found some limpets, then some sea spinach – which tasted wonderful, with the salty tang of the sea. On we went, hunting for rock samphire and sea cabbage, before heading back into Lyme Regis and the sanctuary of the restaurant – by which time we were gasping for breath.

The day unfolded rather well after that. Mark reappeared from putting his fishing tackle away and checking in with his staff. Fortified by a glass of wine, we sat on the deck overlooking the Cobb and basked in the glorious April sunshine. Having been dealt with in the kitchen, the limpets were served with some wild garlic and stonecrop on an unusual fish-shaped platter. 'I've got obsessed with collecting different shaped silver fish platters,' Mark admitted. He assured me that the now cooked limpets tasted a bit like clams but I wasn't convinced. The asparagus tempura, that followed, was delightful though, as were the sweetbreads with wild garlic mayonnaise.

Mark is seemingly a difficult man to pin down. A chef appeared and asked him, 'Are you staying for a little while now or are you here and then gone and then back?' 'Depends,' came the reply. I was glad I wasn't the only one who was finding it tricky knowing what was next on the agenda! Another member of his staff told me you had to be adaptable working with Mark.

Born and raised by his grandparents in West Bay, Mark tries to get out of London and come down to Lyme most weekends. 'I look at it as maybe I was a bit spoiled being brought up somewhere like this when I was younger, just walking down the road and jumping in the sea. And I did love fishing.'

At school he had no idea as to a career. There was the option to do metalwork or domestic science and as he quite fancied the teacher of the latter he and a couple of other boys opted for that. Mark explained further, 'Embarrassingly I got the school prize for domestic science and had to stand up in front of the whole school and collect my Delia Smith cookbook!' He ended up going to catering college at Weymouth. There was a really good lecturer there who would let them go to his flat with the girls and some wine on the afternoons when they were supposed to be broadening their education with other subjects. 'I've always had this thing in my head that the restaurant business should be a bit of fun really.'

Mark then worked at top London establishments and was chef director of Caprice Holdings before setting up his own, enviable empire with the fish house and six other restaurants, soon to be seven, in London, and a town house boutique hotel which has just opened in Lyme Regis. He is very involved in the interior design of his restaurants and likes to add a personal touch by sourcing furniture, plates and details right down to the salt and pepper pots. A lover of art, he sits on the Royal Academy Schools board, and has many friends amongst the 'Brit Art' generation, including Damien Hirst, whose specially commissioned cow and cockerel adorns one of his London restaurants.

He writes columns for *Esquire* and *The Independent* and has written many books on food and cooking. He admits that his hectic timetable is not really conducive

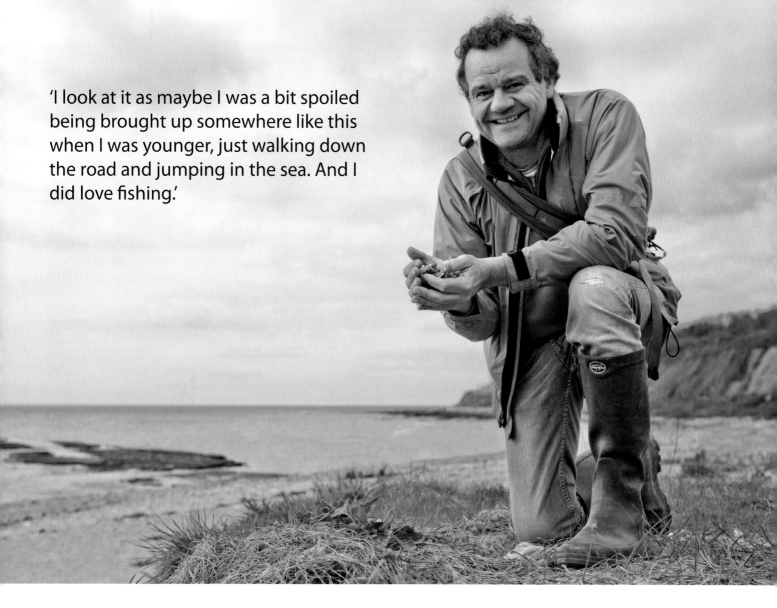

'I look at it as maybe I was a bit spoiled being brought up somewhere like this when I was younger, just walking down the road and jumping in the sea. And I did love fishing.'

to holding down a relationship, with an ex-wife and ex-girlfriends to prove it. I wondered if he would ever retire, though he has only just passed his half century. 'I haven't really thought about it. I don't really think too far ahead. I suppose because of my passion for the business I sort of live and breathe work.'

Mark describes his style of cooking as simple and he lets the ingredients speak for themselves. He doesn't tend to follow trends and quite often he thinks he unintentionally sets one. 'We were the first chicken restaurant, which is quite an obvious thing to do, apart from Nando's.'

Mark, who became more engaging as the interview went on, to the extent that it was hard to leave, really opened up and when we talked about my disappointing attempt at making wild garlic pesto he lit up with enthusiasm and helpful suggestions such as using rape seed oil instead of olive. Having enjoyed his generous hospitality, I agree with Tracey Emin, yet another of his artist friends, Mark Hix is lovely!

# Captain Max Hoskins
## Dorset and Somerset Air Ambulance Pilot

Dorset and Somerset Air Ambulance (DSAA) is a registered charity which receives no direct funding from the Government or National Lottery. It relies on the generosity of the public to help raise the £1.7 million a year it costs to keep flying. The Charity was set up in 2000 and has attended over 10,000

missions since its launch, many of them life-saving.

Their Eurocopter EC135 helicopter, two pilots and servicing engineers are provided by Bond Air Services and are based at Henstridge Airfield, between Sherborne and Shaftesbury. The pilots are Max Hoskins and Phil Merritt.

As a boy growing up in Surrey Max's choice of career was influenced by the nearby Bristow Helicopters training school. He was awarded an RAF flying scholarship and qualified for his private pilot's licence in 1986. He was later sponsored for his commercial helicopter licence by Bristow Helicopters, flying to and from North Sea oil platforms before joining East Midlands Air Ambulance. When he was offered the chance to join Dorset and Somerset Air Ambulance, he jumped at it.

DSAA covers an area of roughly 4,000 square miles, working closely with the other Emergency Services – including the helicopter run by the Coastguard at Portland (now threatened with being replaced by inland services in 2017). Dorset and Somerset Air Ambulance has no winch, so cannot rescue accident victims from the sea or a cliff – though they are regularly called out to the coastal path to rescue those whose walk has 'taken a nasty turn'. Another area where the Air Ambulance plays a key role is in attending riding and road traffic incidents.

The Air Ambulance has priority over all other air transport and has clearance to land anywhere it can safely do so, including your back garden, if on a Helicopter Emergency Medical Service mission. It is also the pilot's decision whether or not it is safe to fly due to weather. Low cloud base is the biggest issue as it means you may not see obstacles. On landing, cables and wires are a hazard and birds can sometimes be an issue. Flying or landing in the wet is not a problem and the helicopter, which cruises at 150 mph, has 'bear paws', big pads on the back of the skids, to spread the weight and stop it sinking on soft ground.

Obviously when the helicopter lands it can draw a big crowd and, if time permits, Max is more than happy to chat to the public, show them the helicopter and answer any questions people may have. 'It's the least I can do. The public deserves an opportunity to find out more because it is they who keep us flying. It's all good PR.'

Through working for the Air Ambulance Max has realised that you have to make the most of your life. 'This job has made me realise that an accident could happen at any time and be just around the corner. You can't get time back, one day it will be too late. So make the most of every day you have.'

# John Hubbard
## Artist

'I make jokes because I like jokes, but art is not a trivial pursuit. It's a serious matter and I am not pleased when it is treated as a subject of levity.'

When Connecticut born John Hubbard first came to live in Dorset with his English wife Caryl, in 1961, nearly everyone around was involved in agriculture. It's now very different, but the beauty of the landscape that originally attracted them is unaltered.

John recalls reading as a child, what he described as a fantastic photographic essay in *Life* magazine on Hardy and Dorset. Aged 30, and living in London, he began discussing with friends where to move to in the country, and Dorset, which had been in his mind, was suggested. A friend in Litton Cheney suggested a rectory in Swyre with three acres which the Hubbards bought for £5,000. After ten years they moved across the fields to where they are now. John has converted a huge dutch barn into his gallery and studio, chickens roam, the views are sensational and the gardens, which are well known, stunning.

He studied at Harvard University where he read Art History and Literature. His father, a lawyer, wanted him to be a writer but John didn't feel he was cut out for writing and discovered art. 'I thought, this is amazing. So much available to be looked at and admired and excited by. So I started art history and remember thinking, I don't know if I'll ever be able to take on Picasso. I was interested in Sienese painting of the 15th century. I firmly believe that if you love art you are not going to get on with everything, but you can find a rationale and interrelationship between things that on the surface appear to be not connected, but are. I love old master paintings and I love Middle Eastern work, so there's a place for all those things.'

After Harvard, John spent three years in Japan with the US Army, during the Korean War. 'I was with counter intelligence, it was great fun, lots of parties.' When he left the army he was 25 and free to follow his passion, attending Art Students' League in New York. It was the 1950s and a small group of American painters had seized the spotlight, creating a style we know today as Abstract Expressionism.

'I found that time exciting, but one of the reasons I came to England was because I found the increasing commercialisation of the art scene in New York very distasteful. A lot of artists went to live outside [New York] to avoid all that. It's a very killing environment – money, money, money, push, push. Overstating things and making false claims and so on.' John went to Italy and then England, which he found much more congenial, which in turn say much about his character.

His early works were inspired by his Dorset surroundings. He tends to work in a sequence and a particular subject occupies him for around five years. 'In that period of time you are following a particular train of thought and seeing, and then it changes. At the moment I am in between; I've just come to the end of one group of pictures [inspired by the quarries in Dartmoor], and I'm looking now for some way to start again. It is a very awkward moment actually.'

Over the decades John has produced thousands of works. Charcoal drawings and oil paintings are his favourite media, but he feels no possessiveness for his art. 'On the whole I like selling, that is the purpose.' He has sold through Marlborough Fine Art gallery in London for 15 years and shows in the US; his work is collected all over the world by private individuals and institutions such as the Arts Council of Great Britain, Tate Gallery and the Victoria and Albert Museum.

John's work can be divided into separate themes; Cornwall, Dorset, Garden, Morocco, Scotland and Spain. He draws inspiration from these places and makes drawings from which he then paints back at his studio – in the old days on large canvasses up to two metres square.

Once 'finished', John puts his paintings to one

side for up to two years. 'I go on adding to them sometimes. Then they go away again, hidden, and I bring them out at intervals and sometimes I see things I want to add to or change.' He was looking through some of his early work recently and found 'a jolly good painting.' It wasn't quite right so he got someone to help him re-stretch it and then John added the final touches. It was sold to the Ashmolean Museum, Oxford and is a large painting called 'Above Lyme Bay'. He didn't mention it was started 1965 and finished in 2012! 'The painting was still the painting of 1965 but it just needed fattening up . . . for slaughter! That can happen.'

I wondered if his style had changed over the years. 'That's a complicated subject because sometimes you can get really cheesed off with your work. Some artists really hate some of the things they've done. They don't admit it, but they do and others should hate it but don't! But I really went off my 60s paintings which were quite different to these [current works]. I had a period of time when I really couldn't bear looking at them.'

John had recently read a book on Picasso and quoted from it. 'Picasso always said that a painting adapts the colouration and the atmosphere of the people who own it.' Thus bad people have a bad effect on paintings and good people have a good effect and John thinks there is a great deal of truth in it. 'There are terrible dealers in the art world who say the most appalling things and behave badly and are crude and vulgar. I make jokes because I like jokes, but art is not a trivial pursuit. It's a serious matter and I am not pleased when it is treated as a subject of levity.'

We discussed some of the better known contemporary artists. I asked what he thought of Damien Hirst's work. 'Richest artist in the world they call him and of course he is not. There are artists far richer than him who just shut up about it. They just count their money and smile!'

John admires the work of Cézanne. 'It would be hard to find a painter of my generation, who is involved in landscape, who wouldn't revere Cézanne. Some people pretend they don't, but it's a pretence. He is the sort of central figure.

'Landscape painting has been considered dead since I started doing it but that's what I want to do. I'm going to carry on and I don't care about being a household name or anything like that. Self expression is not the ultimate purpose of it but it is there to a point. The ultimate purpose is to enlighten and add to the perception of the wonders of life, of the world; a physical visual reality and that is what it's about.'

He doesn't set out with any particular goal but 'just sees how it goes. There are sometimes happy surprises, sometimes disagreeable ones, but on the whole it's been more good things than bad.' He particularly enjoys commissions and loved working at the Royal Opera House, with the rehearsals going on around him, whilst he worked on the backcloth for the sets. He also designed costumes for the Royal Ballet. He taught at Camberwell School of Art in the 1960s, designed a tapestry for the Said Business School in Oxford and the National Visual Arts Gallery in Kuala Lumpur.

This summer he is involved with the Festival of Garden Literature at Petworth House, West Sussex, talking about the relationship between his life as an artist and the garden he has made. He was involved in the running of Tate St Ives, after its initial setting up.

He doesn't sign his work anymore. He used to but realised in the 1960s that it was 'a bit naff.' He added, 'The painting is my signature.'

John has life condensed to a beautiful simplicity. He works hard, he sells paintings. He doesn't feel he is a success, though admits that 'when one had exhibitions and people were consistently buying, that was indicative that something was going right. You were making a connection, conveying something and people wanted it.'

I wondered how he would react if he had to stop painting. 'It could happen. I would cry and sob inconsolably in a room, and then recover. It would be a great deprivation but I would probably look for another outlet – not gardening – can't do much anymore. Thank God that's out of the way!'

# Ted Ingram
## Farmworker and Newspaper Deliveryman

They say that some people live till they are a hundred but die at seventy. This is not true of Ted Ingram. Rarely have I met someone so alive, so sprightly, so kindly and warm with a positive outlook for now and the future, and he is 94 years old.

He greeted us early one morning at the door of the Winterborne Monkton cottage where he has lived for most of his life. At 18 Ted started working on a farm, but the pay was poor. Determined to buy a motorbike with a sidecar, he took on a paper round, delivering the *Dorset Echo* round the surrounding villages.

These days, the *Echo* is delivered to him at 6.30 am. He has his porridge and then goes out on his round in his trusty Peugot, often stopping for a chat or cup of his tea with his granddaughter and some of the others he delivers to. He has no intention of retiring from his paper round, and still finds time to mow the grass on the farm and nearby caravan park.

He showed us memorabilia from his wonderful life: a photograph of him being presented with his long service medal, a certificate from the Royal Agricultural Society of England, his wedding photo of 1949, cards from his birthday on Valentine's Day, pictures of his children and grandchildren – and we couldn't help but notice the wall calendars whose scantily-clad young ladies obviously helped keep the smile on his face!

Despite his small stature, I imagine the arrival of Ted would light up a room. He was a little over five foot until a broken back, a result of falling into a corn silo aged 40, damaged his second vertebra, and now he

claims to be four foot eleven and three quarters. The accident wasn't all bad, he told us, although it would be typical of Ted to see the good in everything. 'Spent five weeks in Weymouth hospital and realised I hadn't had a fag' – so he stopped smoking.

He's clearly lonely after losing both his wife Bet and a daughter, but is lucky to have another daughter, Angela, living close by. 'What I'm trying to do now is get a nice young lady. A companion, so's I could 'ave someone to go out with in the car.' If this wish was ever advertised I have no doubt there would be a queue of applicants eager to spend time with this wonderful old man, who still thinks he's 21, and has the charm to match.

Ted Ingram can probably claim to be the longest serving paperboy as well as the oldest. 'You're famous Ted,' we told him. 'There are pictures of you on the internet.' 'Yeah, that's right!' he said. 'I've 'ad quite a life really; I still 'ave.'

# Leanne Lady Gaga Jackson
## Singer

We were expecting a certain amount of eccentricity when we met Leanne, Lady Gaga, but the mad cackling of Chris and RJ, the Fame Monsters, who were doing their make up in the background, really set the tone for our interview and photo shoot. Chris, who thinks he has ADHD, and RJ who manages the Sea Life Tower in Weymouth, are dancers. But they are game for anything, adding more outrageousness to an already pretty crazy set. They guaranteed attention on Weymouth beach during the photoshoot and if we'd asked them to dance, sing, shout, be naked, I have no doubt they would have obliged. Out of respect for the senior citizens of Weymouth we didn't.

Leanne, by comparison is more composed. She had been singing for years as a solo artist when Lady Gaga came on the scene. She wasn't sure about the music to begin with but lots of people suggested she tried doing a Gaga tribute, so she gave it a go. Word spread quickly. An urgent call from a gay club in Bournemouth meant she had only a week to get costumes and an act together for a gig and it just took off from there. 'I was so nervous, but it was brilliant and I had such a good reception.

'I was soon so into her that all the lyrics were locked in there and I haven't had to do much work learning them.' So into her, in fact, that Leanne has legally changed her name to Leanne Lady Gaga, quite a commitment. 'That would be my dream to meet her. It would be incredible.

'When I'm Gaga I stay in character but I'm not going to embarrass myself doing her accent!' Leanne uses Lady Gaga's exact choreography with her Fame Monsters and studies hours of recordings to get things right. She uses Lady Gaga's phrases at gigs: 'Get your paws up!' 'Now jump!'

'As soon as my glasses go on I can get through a gig,

even if I'm feeling rough. She's a one off pop star. She doesn't care if she looks a bit ugly. I just love her. I'd love to sing with her. Even only one line.'

Leanne is very considered, her house is immaculate and ordered and she is very focused on what she wants. 'I'm a self-taught singer and haven't had any lessons or anything.'

Leanne was born in Bath but has lived in Dorset from the age of seven in Sherborne, then Gillingham, Shaftesbury, and now Weymouth. Though Leanne wasn't *Born This Way* she's doing a very good impression of it.

# Cozmo Jenks
## Milliner

Colourful, zany, alive, individual, bursting with creativity – all words that could describe Cozmo Jenks but not really come close to defining her. You only have to see one of her hats to understand the real depth of Cozmo and her talent. She has had a home in the most idyllic spot near Blandford, completely off the beaten track, for twenty years and lived there full time for the last six. She adores the calmness and healthiness for mind and body, and it is no surprise that what she loves most about Dorset folk is their sense of humour; something Cozmo has in abundance. 'Everything about Dorset is perfect. I don't miss London for a second. I'm the fittest I've ever been, so it's all good really.' She has an artist's perspective and seems passionate in her appreciation of the beauty around her. 'I have to pinch myself every time I come home.'

Having done some stereotypical occupations after school she found herself in Dorchester market aged nineteen and bought some dried teasels and straw with which she made hats. These were all snapped up, and on the back of it she talked her way into an apprenticeship. Since then she has gained an international reputation for her stunning headwear and we found it hard not to rummage through the array of lush ribbons, velvet ladybirds, gossamer butterflies and embellishments of every texture and hue she uses when making them. She has an amazing sense of detail and can judge what will suit someone in the blink of an eye. I never

wear hats; I think I look awful, but in a flash Cozmo popped a creation on my head and even I had to admit I liked what I saw in the mirror. She positioned a sensational beaded cap on Millie which was dazzling. 'Before I even met you I knew that's what would suit you,' she said.

Everything is handmade, so every hat is different. It takes up to eight hours to make each one and she can have ten or more hats on the go at any one time. At the time of writing she was under pressure for the Cheltenham Festival, so was waking up early, walking the dogs and then in her studio by 8am to start blocking hats. In fact we were lucky enough to see her in action fitting Alice Plunkett (*see Alice Fox-Pitt, page 64*) Channel 4 racing presenter, for a deep purple number.

Cozmo is enthusiastic about her hats and also horses, which she breeds. She hunts with the Portman, lives with eleven dogs and is clearly no stranger to having a house full of people and animals. Wonderfully unique and immensely kind, she is clearly a genius when it comes to millinery and her lengthy list of loyal clients, many of them very high profile, are testament to her professionalism. But I wonder if her customers are also attracted by the pleasure of spending time with such a character. You could never describe Cozmo as dull! She has cupboards full of gorgeous, bright, swirly, spotted, striped, patterned, floral, tweeds and tuiles, silks and satins and a shoe collection to die for.

# Emily Kishere

## Playgroup Teacher, Miss Dorset 2013

'If you are just a pretty face and can't talk it's not going to get you anywhere.'

The stunning photograph on the opposite page of Emily Kishere, Miss Dorset 2013, emphasises her beauty. What it doesn't show is how gentle, thoughtful, and down to earth this twenty-three-year-old is.

Emily watched her elder sister, now a model in California, win Miss Bournemouth in 2005 (there wasn't a Miss Dorset competition then) and that, coupled with her desire to 'have a bit of fun,' led to Emily following her sister down the beauty pageant route, with much success. She was the Face of Kent, which led to her qualifying for the Face of Europe at Disneyland. She entered Miss England, having qualified through Miss Dorset, and has also been crowned Miss Bournemouth. She entered Miss Scuba UK this year with great excitement, as the finalists, of which she is one, get to travel to Egypt and learn to dive. She will also get the opportunity to perform a routine, and with a degree from Bournemouth University in Dance, it is this performing side of things that Emily most enjoys. Though she does also love 'getting dressed up, wearing a sparkly dress – who doesn't want to do that?'

She is sponsored for all her hair and beauty needs by Beautifully Gorgeous in Parkstone; not a bad perk when you consider the preening of nails, eyelashes, eyebrows, highlights etc that are routinely required to keep her looking her beauty contest best.

In Miss England, which was in Torquay, the girls had to dress for an Eco round, so Emily designed and made a dress out of Dorset Cereal boxes. There was also a sportswear round, for which Emily made a special effort to get fit, as normally she is lucky enough not to have to stick to an exercise regime. She doesn't need to fuss over what she eats either and claims to 'eat masses' including chocolate and Coke, not known for their slimming qualities.

Of the beauty pageants, Emily tell us, 'Usually it's not bitchy, everyone gets along really well.' She has made good friends from amongst her fellow competitors and judges, who have been very supportive. Emily has judged pageants herself for the juniors and of course will have crowned Miss Dorset 2014 in May.

There are usually no height restrictions for entry, which is just as well as Emily describes herself as 'the shorter end of the pageant girls'. But you must be over 18 and have no children.

Currently, Emily is working as a nanny and playgroup teacher. She has a Diploma in Childcare, and loves working with children, though she would like to get into teaching dance and maybe even put on a pageant one day herself.

Emily tells us that beauty pageants are 'really not all about the way you look these days.' The girl who won Miss England had raised thousands of pounds for the charity Beauty with a Purpose, proving herself to be a fine ambassadress for her country. 'If you are just a pretty face and can't talk it's not going to get you anywhere.'

As well as the criticism, there is also, inevitably, some jealousy that comes with the pageant world but Emily doesn't let it upset her anymore. She says it just comes with the territory, but I suspect she's just too kind to notice.

# John Makepeace OBE
## Designer

'It's really important to be a rebel if you are a designer. I say that because you have really got to reject a lot of what exists.'

The personal statement on the furniture designer John Makepeace's website ends with a wonderful final sentence. 'My passion is to create masterpieces that enrich people's lives and the language of furniture.'

No one could have felt more enriched than Millie and I when we first met John and were taken round his house and garden. Sculpture, paintings and, inevitably, furniture designed by John adorned the space, though the house was not remotely cluttered. Every single item made me think of William Morris's advice: 'Have nothing in your house that you do not know to be useful, or believe to be beautiful.'

John Makepeace is Britain's most distinguished furniture designer. He has been nominated for the Prince Philip Designers prize, and has received Lifetime Achievement Awards from both the American Furniture Society and the Furniture Makers Company. He is an Honorary Fellow of the Arts University Bournemouth, for whom he is currently making a mace, and of Hereford College of Arts.

John is easy to chat to, welcoming and calm. Although modest about his achievements, he is sensible and realistic enough to admit that if his work is to be copied then he would hope people who want the best will still come to him, for the best.

As a child, aged seven, just after the war, John and his family came back to their home near Birmingham to find the house had deteriorated. John remembers seeing the carpenter at work and being given small offcuts of wood, which was still rationed and hard to come by, and being excited by it. 'We had three pieces of furniture at home made by my paternal grandfather and they were better than anything else we had,' John explained. His father was a motor engineer, John told us, 'I think he graduated from making things. I'm a reprobate really, well certainly a rebel. It's really important to be a rebel if you are a designer. I say that because you have really got to reject a lot of what exists.'

He came to Dorset when he bought Parnham House in 1976, and founded the Parnham Trust and the School for Craftsmen in Wood, which provided integrated courses for aspiring furniture-makers. He ran this alongside his own furniture workshops. Over 200 students were trained at Parnham including David Linley, and Konstantin Grcic, the world-famous industrial designer.

'I had resolved that I needed to set up a college to train people in design, furniture making and business,' John said, going on to explain his frustration that one alone of the three is never adequate. 'If you are an entrepreneur you need a variety of disciplines. Business is always a dirty word amongst students. It's the combination of things that actually makes things happen. In education people always think their discipline, whatever it is, is superior to others, and that's not how the world is.' John tolerated maths as a boy but wasn't excited by it, though he thinks it uses the part of the brain that creates good design. 'Later on,' he continued, 'when you can see its relevance you

become responsive and learn quickly.'

It was hard for him leaving Parnham after 25 years, as it was for his wife, Jennie, who had gained a reputation for creating its stunning gardens. But both were in need of a rest from the hard work and endless balancing of the books that running one of Dorset's most celebrated country houses entailed.

We tried John's extraordinarily comfortable chairs. His incredible attention to every aspect of the design, from timber selection, to the shape, to the actual function of the chair and how it will feel, is what makes his work so remarkable. Somehow a chair ceases to be just sat on but something that is good for the posture, easy on the eye and has a fine sense of aesthetic. 'It's a question of taking the trouble and someone being prepared to pay for it,' John explained.

I wondered if he preferred to work in a particular wood, knowing that he often selects the timber for a piece before he designs it. 'I think the answer to that is any wood that I haven't used recently. It's the variety that is wonderful.'

All the wood John uses is indigenous. One stack of 22 feet long planks he showed us, seasoning in his shed, was from an oak, planted at Longleat in 1740 and harvested in 1980.

'The point I want to make is that we use timber cut from trees that belong in our landscape, so that one is actually perpetuating that tree within one's home. I believe that if we want trees, we have got to use our timber, because that is what gives it value.'

# Gail McGarva
## Traditional Boat Builder

Gail was working as a sign language interpreter in Bristol until a journey to the source of the Thames led to a complete change of career. She successfully applied for a City and Guilds Bursary and enrolled at the Boat Building Academy in Lyme Regis in 2005. Walking through the doors she felt she had come home. She became National Trainee of the Year, has collected a certificate from Prince Philip at Buckingham Palace for being Highly Commended in traditional boat building and is thought to be the only female builder of Cornish pilot gigs in the country.

We met in her boat shed in Lyme Regis where she was building *Tempest*, her third gig, and which was successfully launched in 2012. To her, the gig is a way of 'reconnecting people with the sea.' In recent years, gig racing has enjoyed a resurgence, especially amongst women. This year, 2014, 150 teams from all over the world will gather in the Scilly Isles for the World Pilot Gig Championships.

The gigs were originally built to row a pilot out to incoming ships. The first one there got the job and therefore the payment. Her passion for these beautiful 32 foot long craft shines through and she describes their skeletal frame and form with real love. 'It's a form that's evolved through generations rather than being assigned to a museum.'

Gail is powerfully passionate about traditional wooden boat building. Her community spirit and open nature are self-evident, as are her warmth and genuine enthusiasm for what she does.

# Jonathan McGowan
## Eater of Roadkill, Taxidermist

Venison and pheasant are Jonathan McGowan's favourite meats – not a surprising fact until you consider the other options on his menu. He regularly eats roadkill, animals that have been struck and killed by motor vehicles and left on the roadside, and often goes on to stuff the remains of his lunch. Owl, fox, hare, squirrel, badger – 'though they taste like they smell, so I spice it up a bit with lots of curry powder,' he explained.

A rat on the chopping board in the kitchen was awaiting its addition to a stir fry, although we declined Jonathan's kind offer to join him for lunch.

The first unusual thing he ate was a snake; an adder he had found dead when he was a child and wanted to know what it tasted like. He fried it in butter, and though unpleasant it didn't put him off experimenting with other sources of protein.

Jonathan has had a keen interest in wildlife since he was a small boy and loves Dorset for its abundance of animals. 'I couldn't live anywhere else; to be honest, there is more wildlife pound for pound here than there is anywhere in the rest of the United Kingdom,' he told us.

If you are tempted to beat the recession and join Jonathan in his foraging, Dorset apparently abounds in roadkill. He assures us his freezer is always full.

# John McGrath
## Fly Fisherman

We found John fishing for sea bass off Portland Harbour where they follow the squid who come in to spawn. Originally from Yorkshire, John was a gamekeeper on the Trigon estate near Wareham in the 1970s and worked a few years in Sussex before coming back to Dorset. He now works in the Orvis shop in Sherborne and teaches fishing.

He explained, 'Some people you can't teach because they don't listen. They have a preconceived idea and that is as far as it goes. Women are good to teach because they listen and aren't in competition with everything. Men need to cast further than the next man or put more power into it, but the more power you put in just ruins it. It's very gentle, casting.'

John ties his own flies, rarely returning empty handed. 'If I don't catch anything it can be because a change in the weather or something has upset the apple cart. Sometimes you don't fish well for whatever reason – things on your mind perhaps. At other times you know you fished really well and you still haven't caught anything, so you just say "well there are no fish there", then you wonder why.'

I had to ask John what was the biggest fish he had caught. Without the exaggeration one might expect

from a fisherman, he said a seven feet six inch long 350 pound sturgeon he landed in Canada, an experience he described as 'humbling'.

His lifelong passion for the sport started when John was a boy. He was waiting for a fly fisherman to leave the river so he could go worming. Unexpectedly, the fisherman offered him a go and after one cast he was smitten.

The serenity of a fisherman's life has had its moments of excitement, John tells us, chuckling. 'In my 20's I was sat in rushes fishing for bream and all these girls with no clothes on swam right up to me, that was fairly bizarre!' But outwitting the elements and the fish is what is all about.

He has seen shark and seals off Chesil Beach and and occasionally catches mackerel and pollock. He particularly enjoys fly fishing for sea bass because they fight 'like nothing on earth'.

John describes Poole Harbour and Kimmeridge as good fishing, but Portland Harbour is his favourite. 'If you go out there in the morning, before its light, and the sun comes up over the Breakwater, you could be anywhere in the world – fabulous.'

# Father Richard Meyer
Priest

We met Father Richard at the Catholic church of our Lady, Queen of Martyrs, and St Ignatius, a baroque, Italianate church in Chideock. This hidden treasure is quite extraordinary, with beautifully ornate paintings and carving.

Father Richard was brought up an Anglican, converting to Catholicism aged 50. He had been tempted by Catholicism at university but didn't go through with it for fear of upsetting his parents. 'I'd wanted to be a priest since I was about three, but as a Catholic I would never have had a wife and family.'

At Durham University, where he read Theology and History, he fell in love with Jan. In those days, if you were planning to be ordained you had to ask the permission of the Bishop to marry. Permission was granted on condition they waited six years. But they were young and impatient and six years seemed an eternity, so Richard abandoned his plans for ordination, married Jan, became a teacher and had two children.

Finally the call of the church triumphed. He was ordained and went into a series of Church of England parishes for nearly 20 years.

Richard was restless however, 'I got what we call in the trade, "Roman fever".' Finally he obtained permission from Rome to convert to Catholicism and be ordained a priest, which took place in the chapel at Leweston School, near Sherborne, where he was chaplain.

His friends and family were not at all surprised, wondering why he had not converted earlier. 'It was like a secret love affair; something that I always, despite all its faults and failings – which even now are coming to light – just loved from the first time I came across it.'

Father Richard is convinced that being part of a religious community, that traces its history right back to the birth of Christianity, is where he wants to be.

He is now priest at the beautiful church near Bridport, where we met. He was utterly charming and engaging but the only disappointment was that he wasn't wearing his trademark red socks! He was made an honorary Canon of Worcester Cathedral which entitled him – 'if you want to be dressy up about it' – to have red piping round his cassock. Someone suggested he wore red socks to match and this habit has stuck, though he does wear purple on Ash Wednesdays.

The life of a Catholic priest is not dull, Father Richard explained. 'When I hear all this news about people, be it Jimmy Savile or a politician, I am just not surprised anymore, because in the job you know an awful lot about people that no-one else knows, and what humans are capable of. Victor Hugo remarked "there are no bad people, there are only good people who behave badly". It's lovely.'

I asked Father Richard what keeps him in Dorset? 'Well it's where God lives. Have you not discovered? Who wouldn't love it.'

# Joy Michaud
## Chilli Specialist and Vegetable Seed Merchant

With PhDs in Agriculture, Joy and Michael Michaud embarked on a career in horticulture and then bought a plot of land eight doors down from where Joy grew up in West Bexington. They began a nursery from where they produce seeds for the most delicious tomatoes I've ever tasted, as well as loofahs, gourds, other exotic vegetables and countless varieties of chilli.

Over the years they have bred many varieties of their own, giving them names such as 'Yellow Submarine', 'Joker', and perhaps most famously the 'Dorset Naga', considered one of the hottest chillies in the world, with around one million Scoville Heat Units.

In 2013 Joy harvested over 1000 chillies from just one of her Dorset Naga plants and challenged any other grower to exceed that number: as far as I know, no-one got near that extraordinary tally. No doubt 2014 will see even greater success.

Joy is open and honest, and remains baffled by the sudden wave of chilli eating contests, choosing to match each individual chilli to its appropriate use according to personal preference. She suggested lemon mousse with a hint of chilli and persuaded us that anything could benefit from that extra culinary kick.

Polytunnels fill their plot in this idyllic setting with its 180 degree sea views. Perhaps it is the coastal environment, and the amazing amount of light reflected from the sea, that ensure that the produce at Sea Spring Seeds flourishes.

Joy thinks Dorset is proud of their achievements and I would urge anyone even with a passing interest to visit the nursery or buy their seeds – just go cautiously, some are excessively hot!

# Pete Moors
## Hurdle and Furniture Maker

Thirty years in engineering left Pete Moors feeling 'a bit fed up with it'. He was in an office with no windows and couldn't tell if it was sunny or raining. He met someone who had been hurdle making for a couple of years and decided to take a look, visiting him in the woods. Pete was instantly seduced by the environment and the whole process of splitting the hazel rods in two with a billhook, weaving them round upright hazel supports, and so rapidly creating hurdles for use as screens and fences. His enthusiasm grew and he is now making hurdles and furniture from wood full time.

'Hazel is used, as round here it's prolific. I've spent a lot of time helping restore neglected hazel woods to bring them back into the proper cycle, which provides future materials for me and my work, but is also a great benefit for wildlife. When you let in the light and the air, the spring flowers grow really well because previously they were shaded out. In come the insects and birds and all the rest of the wildlife. There is a great pleasure in the fact that I am taking something from the wood but also putting something back.'

Pete also makes tables, lamps, and simple, rustic chairs, selling his furniture through agricultural shows and to collectors.

He showed us a beautiful spalted beech table that was marbled where the fungi had acted after the tree had been felled. The black lines are effectively war zones between the different types of fungus. By working and sealing it, the fungus dies and becomes firm. 'That's one of the wonders of it. When I put a piece of wood on my lathe to make a bowl I can't see what's in there. I haven't got x-ray eyes and usually it's the shape of the log or I'll have some shape in my head, but I don't necessarily know how the bowl will end up.'

Pete regards timber as no different from any other structural engineering material, but as something he can use and make things with. 'Building structures like archways, or houses even, you need to know what wood to use. Oak and chestnut are good for timber frame houses, but certain other woods rot, so you need to know all this and about the stresses and the weights you might be bearing. Although I am no longer a serious engineer I still use my engineering knowledge.'

Pete was born in the Poole Arms on the Quay, 'Born in a pub. Probably die in one as well. Terrible thing I know!' He loves the Dorset coast, Poole Harbour, the Purbecks, the amazing rolling scenery with little fields and patchworks of woodlands.

Here is a man who has found a life and a craft that he is truly content with. As well as working on his own projects, he teaches hurdle making and working with wood at the Dorset Centre for Rural Skills at Farrington (*also see page 30*), and Highway Farm near Bridport.

He is handing on skills about which he is passionate and tries to instil that passion in other people. 'If I can help to bring on a few young people to the industry then fantastic. I had a five year apprenticeship and it's served me really well. There's things I learned then that I am using now still, and it's fabulous.'

'There is a great pleasure in the fact that
I am taking something from the wood
but also putting something back.'

# John Morgan
## Junk Man to the Gentry

John is proud of his 'junk man to the gentry' moniker. He has certainly found an interesting niche in acquiring military and sporting uniforms, luggage, weaponry, items of taxidermy and memorabilia. He then either displays them in his museum, sells them on, or hires them out, often for high profile films and television shows such as 'Downton Abbey'.

He also runs a café from his base in the centre of Shaftesbury and still manages to spend time searching for new stock; he won't consider buying anything on the open market, only privately. Whenever possible, he spends time with his new wife in Germany, skis or plays polo at Tidworth.

John is a member of the Wessex Yeomanry and has had an interest in military uniforms since he was a young boy, often asking his father's friends for badges etc. His shop is bulging with British and ex Colonial items, though not much has survived the hostile climate of India or Africa. There is often termite damage, whilst moths remain a constant and costly hazard. He has opened trunks and found all that is left are the buttons and braid. He values his collection greatly and is reluctant to let items that he can't replace go out for film work or for sale.

As a Liverpool schoolboy, John was told he would most likely come to nothing. 'They said, "Morgan you are useless. You'll be a failure for ever!" It gave me more focus.' He was spurred on to prove his school wrong when an ex-pupil returned in his chauffeur-driven Rolls Royce as a successful adult (he had become publicist for The Beatles). 'Best thing I ever got out of school was knowing that sort of stuff could be done. It was an inspiration.'

With brazen teenage confidence in 1984, aged seventeen, he got a loan from the bank to set up his business and didn't think for one minute that it couldn't work. Two years later he was doing a show in the north-west when some buyers from a London shop asked 'How much for everything?' John suggested what he thought was an outrageous sum, but they didn't blink, buying the lot. On the proceeds he spent a year travelling round the world, after which he went back into business – still confident it would succeed.

John first became interested in taxidermy and hides when he saw a tiger skin in a skip in Mayfair. 'I thought, that's wrong. You can't do that. So I just had it out of the skip, cleaned it up and let it out a few months later for film hire.'

John moved to Dorset in 1991. He loves the people. 'They are free spirits and welcoming, and still with a sense of humour. The landscape is sensational. No compunction whatever to live anywhere else but Dorset. This is the place to come home to.'

# Oswald Morris OBE, DFC, AFC, BSC
## Cinematographer

During Ossie Morris's long and distinguished career as a cinematographer he was often 'lumbered with Richard and Elizabeth [Burton])'. As well as being close friends, they generously paid for the reception at the wedding to his second wife, Lee, in Rome. Ossie obviously had a wonderful rapport with the many famous actors and actresses he filmed and his whole manner conjured the glamorous era of 1960s and 1970s filmmaking – of which Ossie was clearly an important part.

Ossie was determined to become involved with films as a young boy, but breaking into the industry wasn't easy. He was at the point of giving up when he was called up for military service on the outbreak of war in 1939. He was seventeen when he first put on the pale blue of his Royal Air Force uniform, eventually joining Bomber Command as a pilot flying Lancasters, and winning both a Distinguished Flying Cross and Air Force Cross.

Ossie moved to Dorset in 1976. Whilst filming *Goodbye Mr Chips* at Sherborne School in 1969 he had taken a bungalow at Tolpuddle and fallen in love with the county, and decided he would retire here. He was President of the Blandford Film Society and was still very much involved with the film world well into his 90s.

A fastidious man, who had everything in order, we were surprised and thrilled when he allowed us to handle his impressive collection of awards, amongst them an OSCAR and three BAFTAS. It was impossible to say which was his favourite film of all those that he had made, as the list is so long and includes *The Guns of Navarone, Oliver, Fiddler on the Roof, Moulin Rouge, Lolita, The Wiz*, and *The Man with the Golden Gun*.

Oswald Morris loved Dorset and its beautiful countryside and died peacefully at his cottage in Fontmell Magna in March 2014.

# Barbara Murray
## Dog Breeder, Shower and Judge

From the moment Ozzy was born, Barbara Murray knew he was a Champion. Black and tan, smooth-haired, griffon bruxellois are rare and this, together with his construction and temperament, have gained him prize after prize, including Champion at Crufts.

However amazing his achievements, Barbara is not at all fussy about her top dog, or any of the other thirteen she had in the house: 'all these little noisy things'. But they are very much part of the family and although she admits she likes to win, she doesn't take it too seriously and enjoys her hobby. It's a labour of love and she travels as far as Scotland, Blackpool, Darlington and Leeds, often leaving early in the morning and coming back late at night. Showing dogs is a tiring and costly process. The prize money is negligible (a £100 at Crufts) but you do get given dog food – a year's supply if you win – and of course there's the kudos.

'I'm not breeding anymore as I am getting on a bit (she is in her early 70s). I am just showing. We came here in 1964 and I've been showing dogs since 1966.' Barbara was born in Germany, her husband worked in London and they came to the West Country at the weekends as he had family in Lyme Regis. Now she lives here full time and describes Dorset as lovely. 'The sea, downs, hills in the south and the north – all quite different.'

Barbara is also a judge of show dogs, which has taken her all round the world as well as to Crufts, which she has judged twice.

When she started showing she knew she didn't want to go with something that wasn't any good so she had a couple of 'little ones' which got the odd second and

third prize, and then this dog, Ozzy, came along and she decided, 'I have to show him, because he is so outstanding'.

'I've done dogs for nearly fifty years now, so I think it will soon be time to pack up.' She may well do so, but as everybody tells her, she will miss them.

# Charlie Newman
## Publican and Cider Maker

Whether it be for a post-walk pasty . . . or to sample Charlie's cider, a journey to the Isle of Purbeck would not be complete without a visit to the Square and Compass.

Considered by many to be Dorset's finest public house, the Square and Compass in Worth Matravers oozes character. From the hatch that serves as the bar, the panelled walls, stone floor and atmospheric fire, through to the regulars, without which no decent pub is complete, it is the sort of place where you feel instantly welcome.

Charlie, whose grandfather, Charles, took over the pub in 1907 is determined to change it as little as possible and, apart from the addition of the delightful fossil museum, he has kept it the same. He bought the freehold in 1994 a year after his father, Ray, died and then they had a party for about ten years! Charlie laughs, 'Now I'm all sensible!'

'This pub can tick quite a few boxes,' he told us, explaining that customers come after the easy circular walks nearby, or by bicycle, after climbing – even after walking the coastal path from Durdle Door or Old Harry. The pub is as well known for its live music as its pasties, with bands playing their own songs, not covers.

Charlie makes cider in a barn round the back, about 24,000 litres this year, and to his knowledge has only ever had one pint returned, so he must be doing something right. Ale is obviously the mainstay of the pub's drinking menu but there is never any cider left over.

He makes three types, a dry 'Eves Idea', medium 'Sat down Beside 'er' and sweet 'Kiss me Kate', which obviously we had to sample just to be sure. No sooner had I remarked that this rather delicious clear, clean liquid didn't seem that alcoholic, than a warm glow hit me and I realised that sampling cider at three o'clock in the afternoon was yet another perk of researching this book.

Charlie began cider making a decade ago after acquiring an old twin-screw press. For fun they set it going and held some demonstration days at the front of the pub. It was powered by a tractor and a great big leather belt, 'Health and safety would have shot me!' Charlie says. After a couple of years of this fairly makeshift set up, Charlie decided to take it seriously. He is passionate about his cider-making and has a sound scientific knowledge of the processes involved.

He manages an orchard locally and harvests the fruit from its 140 trees. He also accepts apples from locals, buys in some from a Dorset grower, using varieties such as Chisel Jersey and Dabinette. It's physically demanding and what Charlie enjoys is that it's a 12 month cycle and by the end of it they are absolutely exhausted. With the help of some really good lads, he presses about 200 tonnes of apples over 6 back-breaking weeks.

Charlie also has a smallholding; he has seven Dexter cows, three Iron Age pigs which he explained are 'wild boar cross Tamworth, really hairy and quite wild', seventy ducks, chickens and bantams, three geese and six dogs.

He is also a keen fossil-hunter. 'I don't really set out to go fossiling,' he said. ' I go to take my dogs for a walk and never come home empty handed. It's just the pleasure of finding something; it's that little reward for a journey.'

Most of his finds end up in the pub museum and he shares more interesting items with other enthusiasts, including his sister who comes each week. Charlie links up with Steve Etches, whose fossil collection is renowned in Dorset, indeed globally, for his incredible knowledge of palaeontology, even though he is an amateur. Steve has donated his collection, probably one of the best in Europe, to a purpose-built museum in Kimmeridge which is due to open in 2016.

Charlie's mother's family, the Smiths, were farming nearby from the mid 17th century, 'So we haven't gone far, have we? I like the fact things have gone almost full circle. This pub is very important to me and to lots of other people.' Whether it be for a post-walk pasty, a stop off on the way back from the beach or to sample Charlie's cider, a journey to the Isle of Purbeck would not be complete without a visit to the Square and Compass.

# Martin Oliver
## Great Dorset Steam Fair

We were lucky enough to secure a fifteen minute chat with Martin Oliver, son of Michael, founder of the Great Dorset Steam Fair, also known as 'The National Heritage Show', on the day before the 2013 fair opened at its regular site in Tarrant Hinton. After eleven busy months of preparation, Martin and his staff were ready to host one of Europe's largest events for the 45th year.

'They (the steam engines) probably look better now than they did eighty or ninety years ago,' Martin told us as we stood by the immaculate coachwork of *Dolphin*, 'Gorgeous isn't it, all the way from Aberdeen.'

The time and dedication put in by these enthusiasts is extraordinary. They invest a considerable amount of money keeping their engines in pristine condition and some are valued at a million pounds. The vehicles and steam-powered vehicles, tractors and farm machinery are displayed in an area covering 600 acres. Also on site are classic cars, commercial vehicles, shire horses, rustic crafts and bygones collections. There is a market, live music, funfair (some of which is steam-powered), displays of heavy haulage, threshing, log-sawing, ploughing, road making and steam rolling. In 2013 a new Guinness World Record was set at the Steam Fair for the largest parade of steam rollers; 103 vintage rollers in all.

The GDSF even has its own radio station, Steam Fair FM, which broadcasts for the duration of the show, usually over the August Bank Holiday weekend, and a day or two either side.

The show attracts up to 200,000 visitors and with 30,000 people on site at any one time it makes the fair the fifth largest population centre in Dorset. If that doesn't put it into perspective, the ten miles of electric cable needed or 200 tonnes of coal and 550 barrels of beer consumed might show the scale of the operation.

Martin lives in Child Okeford where his family have lived for over a thousand years. 'We're farmers and there's been a son every generation. Tom, Martin's youngest son, is picking up the ropes now, Martin tells us, 'He's been with me every minute of every day since we've been on site here.'

Martin added, 'Dad started in 1968, nothing more than a village fête basically and this is the fourth site we've been on, but we're only four miles from where it started. We've got some guys over from New Zealand this year, Africa, the States, Holland, all over. Not just visitors, exhibitors. The net is such a fabulous tool you can just reach all corners these days. It's a steam and vintage and heritage event plus everything else we've got here with the music festival. There's nothing quite like it.

'My dad always said keep the informal atmosphere when people are walking around. Behind the scenes there are all sorts of risk assessments taking place but inevitably, with an event this size, you are going to get some problems, but hopefully not too many.'

# Steve Oxford
## Artisan Baker

'Quite something isn't it?' Steve declared. We were peering at the 95-year-old steam tube oven recently converted from oil (originally wood and faggots, then coal) to bio fuel, specifically wood pellets, at Oxfords Bakery in Alweston.

Was it Steve's engaging personality and friendly banter or the promise of cake that kept us enthralled in his bakery for most of the morning. It is all too easy in this day of convenience and rushing about to forget just how fantastic a humble loaf of bread can be. Simply made, in a traditional way, with no fuss and nothing but water, flour, yeast and salt, lots of love and an old hot oven. That's before we get onto Belgian buns or Eccles cakes, lardy cakes and wholemeal loaves hot to the touch. Steve explains it is because of his father's stubbornness that they have continued to bake in the same way for the century the business has been going. And suddenly it is fashionable to bake, and to bake well, and Steve's making the most of it.

He showed us an extremely rare single rotary arm Jones dumbrill mixer which is used every Friday night, to make two batches of white bread. It has been used in exactly the same way since the 1960s, when they only made white loaves which were delivered door to door in Morris 1000 vans. We were rather taken with this mixer and Steve gamely agreed to be photographed in it.

The bakery also has a steam-powered oven which gets wheeled out every year at the Great Dorset Steam Fair. They have used the same flour from Stoates in Cann Mill (*see page 140*) since the business began and on their 100th birthday Steve commissioned a new dough bin from the local joiners, F Cuff & Son, who had made the original.

Despite inheriting these wonderful artisan baking ways, Steve is also progressive, organising farmers' markets and running breadmaking courses. He had

recently broken the world record for the biggest Victoria sponge, which measured a massive 5 feet across and 15 inches deep. He has opened new outlets in Sherborne, Blandford and Canford Cliffs, and feels his main contribution to the family business has been his willingness to try something new. 'Dad

acknowledges that I'm moving things forward a little bit. He's got a set of reins and I can feel that tugging now and again.'

So overwhelmed were we by Steve's chat, the warmth of the oven and smell of freshly baked scones that we forgot to talk about Dorset and what Steve loves about it, but really I think Dorset should be asking that question of Steve. What do we love about Oxfords Bakery? For me it's the lardy cake, especially since Steve told me most of the lard runs off during cooking so it's probably not fattening at all!

# Jeremy Pope
## High Sheriff of Dorset 2012/2013

Jeremy Pope was High Sheriff of Dorset for 2012/13, the nomination of which is wildly comic and improbable, in his opinion. Holders of the 1,000 year-old office get nominated about five years in advance and put on a roll. In March of the year the appointment begins, the Queen makes the formal appointment by actually pricking the velum roll of the names (in nomination) against the name of the person who is next to be High Sheriff.

'You cannot say "I am going to be the next High Sheriff" until the pricking ceremony is finished, which is a bit arcane as you are meant to be getting yourself all ready for it and it doesn't work frightfully well. If you sin or decide you don't want to be High Sheriff, you get removed from the roll,' explained Jeremy.

A lot of the Sheriff's power was eroded when Henry VII appointed the first Lords Lieutenant as the Crown's representative in counties. The current role is as the Sovereign's representative in the county for matters relating to the Judiciary and the maintenance of law and order. Jeremy's professional career as a solicitor no doubt helped, but 'It's pretty full on, so a year is plenty.' Jeremy has since been replaced by Mrs Catriona Payne and Mrs Jane Stichbury.

Jeremy is particularly fascinated by the geological diversity of Dorset, and tells us 'it's got effectively virtually the entire gamut of geology of the UK with the exception of the igneous rocks.'

# Cath Pratley
## Willow Basket and Coffin Maker

Although Cath gave up the travelling life some years ago, in favour of a more permanent residence in a charming cottage near Lydlinch, there are elements that are evocative of her Romany-style years on the road; a dog chained up outside the house, wind chimes in the trees and the kettle boiling away on the sitting room stove.

Cath gave birth to all her three children at home; Rose, in a gypsy caravan in the midst of winter, Jim was also born in a caravan and Ruby in a bender, which is a kind of tent, on the common at Shaftesbury.

Outsiders have the preconception that travellers live in cold conditions, but it's not true, assures Cath, as the fire was always going and everyone was warm, clean and comfortable. Her son has left home now but her girls live with her and Rose is the one responsible for Cath's striking hair style, a nod to her punk days and the quirkiness with which she describes herself.

It was whilst living on a horse-drawn site in the Forest of Dean that Cath started weaving willow. The kids went to school and she got to work, selling her wares through farmers' markets. From baskets Cath moved on to willow coffins and trained under a Master Basketmaker. She now runs workshops in the

summer and sells at woodfairs, festivals and summer shows.

All the willow comes from Weston Zoyland on the Somerset levels and is cut in January. The willow she uses varies in colour, depending on its treatment once it has been cut, and the finished result is beautiful, as well as environmentally friendly, a sensible option for a burial or cremation. She also makes cribs and Moses baskets. When Cath dies she would like to be cremated and have her ashes put in a willow Viking longship and be floated out to sea.

Cath has had some interesting orders for her biodegradable, made-to-measure willow coffins. Her most recent commission is awaiting delivery to a lady who intends storing it in her attic until needed. Another customer commissioned a pink coffin, a request which involved dyeing the white willow and rope.

An average coffin can carry a body of up to 22 stone and is reinforced with plywood, which also keeps the bottom smooth; you wouldn't want a rough edge of willow poking out and catching on the rollers at the crematorium, or whilst sliding into a hearse. The coffins take about four days to complete and are lined with a natural canvas waterproofed with wax, though some people ask for special linings such as tweed. She assured us that the materials used are opaque enough to prevent the silhouette of the body from being seen.

# Margaret Ralph
## Game Dealer and Deer Stalker

Despite her advancing years, Margaret Ralph is active and nimble. Her passion for wildlife and country pursuits come across clearly and with her gentle voice and interesting stories, she is a pleasure to chat to.

Margaret first became interested in shooting for the pot when walking the hedgerows with her father as a young child. Money was short. They learned to butcher their own meat and catch rabbits and other wild game. She used to go out ferreting and then took up shooting in her teens.

Decades on, Margaret's way of life has barely changed and people bring in rabbits, deer, pheasants and all manner of game for her to deal with and store in her refrigerated larder, and she still goes out with a gun herself regularly. It isn't uncommon for her to find a deer left on her doorstep when she gets up in the morning, such is her reputation as the local game dealer

'I shoot an' all that. People say I got this and it wants dealing with. You need to know what you are

doing, so death is instant. I don't like to see things suffer.'

A true countrywoman, she has a great love of the rural life and nature. She appreciates the variety of landscape in Dorset and the characters it contains – then came a broad grin as it suddenly dawned on her, 'As you get older you realise you're one of them!'

We took a look at the game larder humming away in her yard. It contained the carcasses of at least eight deer along with countless game birds. She picked up a tupperware container filled with fresh offal, 'Do you like kidneys?'

I'm sure Margaret's laughter wasn't a response to our squeamishness, she's not that kind of person, but she had every right to chuckle about people like us who move from London to the country and feel we've really settled, yet still reel from such sights. Those of us who have only lived in the country for a decade might be considered townies, but that is certainly not a word you could use to describe Margaret Ralph.

# John Randall

## Chairman, Dorset Down Sheep Breeders Association

We tried to persuade John Randall, a true gentleman and one of the country's most knowledgeable people when it comes to sheep, to wear a rosette for the photograph; we'd selected one from his box containing about a thousand. He declined to pin it to his lapel explaining 'Biggest amateur cock-up you can make. I'm a professional, my dear!'

Sheep breeders and the show ring have obviously kept him entertained over his lengthy career as a breeder and judge, and he is proud of his flock of Dorset Down sheep, from the same strain for over sixty years.

At nearly ninety years old, John is still involved in the world of sheep, 'I help quite a bit with the annual show and sale and flock competition. Can't do so much as I did, as I can't get about.' He still judges on various panels but doesn't like to be called an expert, describing it as 'a horrible word!' John reckons he must have judged at every show in the South of England and Midlands over the years, and at least four times at the Royal Show.

He has been involved in agriculture ever since he left school, and spent his holidays as a boy at his uncle's farm, helping out with the milking. His father was a wheelwright, carpenter and undertaker and he told John and his older brother, 'Do whatever you want to in life. But whatever we chose to do he expected us to do it properly.' Their neighbour, Percy Warren, kept a flock of sheep and it was this flock that sparked John's life-long enthusiasm for all things ovine.

John Randall doesn't only have a passion for Dorset Down sheep; he also kept a highly successful flock of South Downs when he was in Sussex. These have even denser wool than the Dorset 'like a felt.' He won the South Down championship at the Royal nine times 'Put it like this. Randall's name is on there [the cup] more times than anybody else!'

People have often asked him how long he spent getting a sheep ready for showing. 'Five months before the lamb was born' was his answer. In other words it's all in selecting the right parents. He produced a video in 1996 'Preparing Sheep for Show' and has written two books, his autobiography, *Wattle Hurdles & Leather Gaiters*, and *Mary Ann the Lady Farmer*, a novel about a Somerset cheesemaker.

He told us how, in the old days, when sheep needed transporting they'd simply tie them up in the corner of the guards' van on the train. If they were going up to Scotland they'd be there the next day. The sheep were weighed first and if they were more than 140 pounds the costs rose. John sold rams to Willie Whitelaw, the politician, for years. 'He was a character; could drink bloody whisky too!'

Sheepdogs have played a big part in John's life and he explained that he always had two collies working, which were never for sale, and two more coming on which were, and added nicely to his income. 'I'm a bit different I think, to some people, as I always think when you come in in the evening, and you've had a hard day, you want somewhere comfortable for a lie down. Our dogs always came in at the evenings and slept in the house, but in the back. Always.'

'I'm a bit different I think, to some people, as I always think when you come in in the evening, and you've had a hard day, you want somewhere comfortable for a lie down. Our dogs always came in at the evenings and slept in the house, but in the back. Always.'

# Ben Ronaldson

## Real Tennis Professional

By his own admission Ben is from Real Tennis Mafia. His mother, father, uncle, cousin and brother are all involved and in a sport with only a few thousand players that's quite a domination. Both his parents have been World Champion, so it's clear where his talent came from.

It's a complex game and, according to Ben, takes

the prolonged nature of the rallies, which can range from 2-20 shots, with the balls travelling at up to 130 mph.

People come from as far as London to play in Dorset, for the county is lucky enough to have two real tennis courts. The one in the east of the county is at Canford School, where Ben was educated, and his uncle, Steve, is the real tennis professional.

Ben was photographed at the court at Walditch, near Bridport, which was originally built in 1885 by the owner of the estate, Joseph Gundry, of the Bridport netmaking family, in the hope that the Prince of Wales would come and play. Unfortunately he didn't. Nor it seems did many others after Gundry's death in 1891. The court ended up neglected and then being used for many different activities, including roller skating.

During the Second World War it was requisitioned by the Americans and used as a garage, who made a large hole in the end wall to allow the vehicles access. After the war, it became a cowshed and eventually fell into disrepair. It was renovated and reopened by the Bridport and West Dorset Sports Trust in 1998.

Ben was at Hampton Court before Walditch and has played on all but three of the UK's 27 courts. Jesmond Dene in Northumberland, Fairlawne in Kent and Falkland Palace, an extraordinary open-air court in Fife, Scotland, still elude him, but aged just 38, Ben has plenty of time to complete the set.

The game is still played with wooden racquets and handmade balls, something each pro like Ben will produce painstakingly in spare moments. Starting with crushed up cork, wrapping and winding further layers of an old ball, webbing and string, and then finally stitching two bits of felt to produce slightly imperfect but beautifully erratic balls. When you play you hire the 72 balls that are on the court. One set lasts two or three weeks, so it's a real labour of love.

'I dread to think how many thousands of balls I've made in my life but you don't realise you are doing it after a while,' Ben explained. 'When we mark matches we are sitting there making them, so it doesn't really get in the way.' As each one takes well over half an hour it is just as well!

about two years to learn how 'to be pretty bad', so requires commitment. 'Eccentricity ties in with playing this game! Most people playing here have something a little bit wrong with them, including me!'

One of the best things about the game is that the top players keep going. Real Tennis has been described as like watching a war of attrition due to

'My Dad said "You'll never be wealthy but if you work hard and keep your nose clean you'll earn a living"'.

# Clive Samways
## Fish Merchant

Samways was set up by Clive's father, Clifford, over 50 years ago. Clifford had a van, fished part-time and sold his own catch on West Bay quay. Things have come a long way since Clive took over in 1985, when he was eighteen, and his father retired to look after Clive's dying mother. Now they enjoy a multi-million pound turnover, employ over seventy employees, and have good relationships with the hundred or more boats they buy from, which, Clive tells me, is really key.

'I never intended to come into fish, at all. Civil engineering interested me. I had lots of plans for my life, but they didn't involve fish. From eleven years old I was always on the stall so I knew my fish, and could fillet, but I never intended to go into the business.'

'My Dad said "You'll never be wealthy but if you work hard and keep your nose clean you'll earn a living" and so I got involved.'

But it hasn't always been easy. A major skiing accident in 2006 left Clive with brain damage, hearing and memory loss. He has had to relearn most of his encylopedic knowledge of fish. At one stage he did not even know how to use a telephone. The specialists advise him to work only an hour a day, but on the day we met he had arrived before six in the morning, and was due to leave thirteen hours later – the business is his, and his wife Sarah's, passion.

'I love seafood and everything that we manage to do. We've gone from £100,000 a year turnover to edging £12 million at the moment. So it's quite a

change.'

Clive's favourite fish depends on the time of year, because you have to eat to the seasons. 'This time of year (early March), you've got to go a long way to beat pollock. In another month when it warms up I wouldn't touch them. But May, June, July go for a flat fish, probably brill or a really big turbot. I like some of the sustainable fish. Gurnard's one of the best: they are good in all seasons. John Dory is fantastic. So they would probably be my favourites.'

Clive loves his home county, especially the coast road to Weymouth behind the Fleet to Abbotsbury. But he summed it up by saying 'Dorset was the unknown county for so many years. Now it's been found.'

# Sam Scriven

## Earth Science Advisor for the Jurassic Coast

Sam Scriven was born in Weymouth and studied Geology at Plymouth University. He always thought he wanted to work in a museum and his job as Earth Science Advisor for the Jurassic Coast, in charge of scientific communication and conservation, isn't that different from museum life. 'My job really is nature conservation; a bit like the Dorset Wildlife Trust, just with rocks!'

Sam trains teachers to relay information about Geology and the Jurassic Coast. His department runs workshops in schools and occasional field trips: 'But mainly we leave that to the people in the coast centres and field centres. Our work at a strategic level is to look after the Jurassic Coast, making sure there aren't any inappropriate developments. Coastal defences must be done in the right way, because we have to have them to protect bits of towns that might fall into the sea.'

They also deal with new fossil finds, assist with projects that interpret and promote the coast and advise on new museums.

We photographed Sam near Portesham, at a place known as Rocket Quarry, sitting on a fossil tree or, to give its correct technical name, Algal Burr, which is where algae has deposited layer upon layer on a tree that has become submerged, and essentially fossilised in those algal layers. Amazingly, you can still see the outline of the original 145 million year old tree and the texture of the bark, running through the centre of this ridged, enormous maggot-like mound.

Sam explained. 'No flowering plants or anything like that existed here at that time so it would have been a conifer – something like a monkey puzzle maybe. My own job brings me inland which is why I have brought

you here. The coast gets an awful lot of attention. Places like this tie into the whole aesthetic of Dorset; the look of Portesham is completely based on the building stone that was available for people to use, and that is part of geological conservation. Accessing the scientific resource of the geology is contingent on being able to dig it up. It doesn't have to be done on an enormous scale, that destroys wildlife and that sort of thing. Quarrying is part and parcel of geology and generally considered a good thing, after all without it we could not enjoy beautiful villages built out of stone.'

The other advantage to the geologists is that the quarrymen can alert them to any interesting finds. 'There was a good illustration of that on Portland, four years ago. They found a fossilised turtle in one of the quarries. We cut out an enormous block containing the 35 centimetre fossil and it was taken away, prepped and now it's in Portland Museum.'

It was a privilege to meet someone so fascinating and knowledgable about his subject, and Sam is easy going with wonderfully optimistic views. On landslides, for example, he considers the recent and dramatic slip near Lulworth Cove as just a refreshing of the coastline and nothing to be concerned about – 'all part of the natural erosion of the coast'.

I asked him where was the best place to Dorset. He replied, 'Well I don't know, is there one? I feel very lucky to live here and sometimes feel a bit smug when I go elsewhere. It makes me very demanding as a holidaymaker! With 95 miles of coastline and a whole county to run around in, Dorset is great. I wouldn't want to be anywhere else.'

# The Earl of Shaftesbury
## Landowner

'I was just Nick, a DJ and music promoter, and that's what people knew me for.'

Nick Ashley-Cooper, the 12th Earl of Shaftesbury, is not one to shy away from a challenge. Running through deserts, establishing a techno music scene in New York in his early 20s, recovering from damaging his spinal cord in a riding accident and, more recently, undertaking the monumental restoration of his family home, St Giles House in Wimborne St Giles, are all things he takes in his stride. He is relaxed and welcoming and admits he still pinches himself every morning when he wakes up in his stunning surroundings.

St Giles House was built in 1650 with later additions, and Lord Shaftesbury and his German wife, Dinah, together with their young son and daughter, originally just wanted to make a home there for themselves. Somewhere along the way this simple aim has ended up in a multi-million pound restoration project of the house and grounds.

Nick's destiny has been determined in part by misfortune; he tragically lost his father, the 10th Earl, and brother, the 11th, within a few months of each other in 2005. After their deaths, which led to Nick inheriting the St Giles Estate, and the responsibilities that went with it, he went to business school in London for two years, having left New York where he was working as a DJ. 'After the personal tragedy in my family I felt if I went straight here it would be too much. So I immersed myself in work that I knew would be useful in the long run.'

He hopes his son Anthony, now three, will be able to experience as much of life as possible outside of the estate, before he takes on the role of running it. Nick is very grateful that he had the chance to do that himself, whilst in New York in the early 2000s. 'I was absolutely passionate about my DJing. I started doing nights in Manchester, where I went to university, and I just set about trying to meet as many people as I

could. I bumped into a promoter who was running a big club in New York and he brought me over to manage it. I was in charge of 20 security men from the Bronx when I was about 24 – completely ridiculous looking back at it, but that got me in and my foot in the door. As I came from the European scene and knew what was going on here, especially in Germany, we started bringing over artists and established a scene in New York, which was great and all about timing really. It's a pretty tough world in one sense, long hours, all night and during the day – pretty draining, but those people who have stayed in that world, who I keep in touch with, are doing fantastically well now because the whole scene has just exploded in America. You have kids in their early 20s playing Las Vegas and flying in private jets – it is totally nuts!

'It was quite fun to pluck some of my friends who were still very much immersed in the music scene in New York and bring them down to deepest Dorset, when we got married here. It was quite a thing and a lot of them had no idea about all this in my family because I never really talked about it. I was just Nick, a DJ and music promoter, and that's what people knew me for. I still don't feel special, though it is quite a unique set of circumstances, but actually it suits me because I like life to be interesting and challenging and I suppose, in a weird way, I am quite cut out for what has happened.'

The house and gardens at St Giles are impressive, but Nick has the admirable ability to treat them as a home not a museum and is looking forward to sharing them with others. Their first event was the Grand Shaftesbury Run, which this year attracted 400 runners. As a keen runner himself, particularly over long distances in challenging conditions, that may have been the inspiration for this event, though since his riding accident he has lost a lot of his strength and

his running is affected.

In his ultra running days he took part in events in spectacular locations (eg the Sahara, Gobi and Atacama deserts). 'The reason they are so addictive is that they give a sense of complete freedom; in some of the races you have to carry all your food, equipment, clothes etc. There is a definite sense of trying to explore what your personal limits are in a physical way and then it also becomes quite a mental challenge too. You find that you can do way more than you thought you could. It has been good for me and taught me not to get blinded by the finish line or the impossible task of where you have got to go, just concentrate on the next bit. You just chip away. It's been the same with the house. We have still got a lot to do but we have achieved way more than we thought possible.

'It's been quite a journey, but at least I now know where everything is. It is ordered in my head even though it is not visually. Some rooms are still quite chaotic but I know what I am dealing with and I feel we have picked everything up and put it down, if you know what I mean. If I look back at some of the photographs of before we started [restoration] I think, God I must have been mad, but it is great now to be where we are, so we don't have to face that decision again.'

Last winter's storms were particularly challenging. 'I'd been going round telling everyone the house was weather-proof but water started coming in in five or six different places and I was running out of towels. At that point I was cursing myself for living in such a bloody big house! We needed one hundred towels to cover all the leaks!

'We are in a rather fortuitous position that we get to see how others have done it. There are lots of great stories of estates being turned around, and in a way you have seen a real resurgence of these old houses and beautiful parks, and people are starting to love them again. They appreciate the challenge of keeping them maintained and the importance of having them around. It is making it easier for us to keep going.'

Nick is justifiably proud of his forebears and their achievements. Notably the 7th Earl of Shaftesbury, a social reformer and philanthropist whose life and work are commemorated by the Shaftesbury Memorial Fountain at Piccadilly Circus,

better known as Eros. An exact copy of the statue, made from the same mould, graces the sunken garden in Dorset and points exactly towards its counterpart in W1.

The wonderful mix of traditional values and respect for the past and a more modern approach to life are perhaps personified, not only by Nick's earlier career as a DJ but by his tattoos. He has a large tattoo on the inside of his right forearm composed anatomically of nuts and bolts, signifying 'Robots', the name of the parties he ran in New York. 'I wanted something to anchor me to what my life was at that time and it encapsulates everything up to that point, so if I'm starting to get too stuffy I just look at it.'

Another, on his left shoulder, is of Psyche and Eros, a nod to the 7th Earl and the charitable work he did in his lifetime. 'He is a big inspiration for the family. My point of getting the tattoo was to think well if there was someone who can do that much good in

my family then I should be able to at least contribute something positive, even if it is a little tiny smidgeon of what he has done. I've got a tattoo of an ant over my chest which represents my brother [Anthony] who passed away. They all carry a story and something that is important to me. I must get one of Dorset!'

It is no surprise that Nick, with his easy manner and relaxed approach, has been welcomed back by all those in the village and on the estate. It must be invigorating for them to see the house restored and improved, the gates thrown open, and a young family enjoying all that St Giles has to offer. From what has been a difficult period in the history of the Shaftesbury estate it seems that, under Nick's guidance and with his amazing spirit and unshakeable determination, the future is bright.

'We are up and running now and we have just started to do weddings, anniversaries, speaker events, parties. I want to try and create something here that is more than just another stately home doing generic type events. I want to instil a feeling that there is a meaning to coming here, that is connected to some of the stories of my ancestors and the feeling and the magic of the park. That is the next challenge – how to create that.'

# Emsie Sharp
## Glass Blower

It takes a long time to perfect the technique of successful glass blowing but after twenty years Emsie Sharp has cracked it, if you'll forgive the pun.

She trained at Farnham Art College, but after a spell in the 'hot shop' was hooked on the art of glass blowing and now commands decent prices for her beautifully fine tableware, lamps and abstract work. 'As soon as I tried it that was it, but it takes a long time to be really good, so you have to persevere.'

She spent three years in Venice where the work is on a much larger scale, allowing the glass blowers to have up to 12 pots of different coloured glass melting away in the volcano-like furnace. Emsie uses clear glass, adding colour from colour blocks, like sticks of rock, arranged neatly in her studio.

Her work is sold through fairs around Christmas, as well as to customers far and wide. Much of her work is bought as wedding presents. She does some teaching too. She explained of her art, 'You've got to be in control of it. You need an assistant, you can't make glass on your own. It is very quick, takes only 10 to 12 minutes but is very intense and things can go wrong.'

It is a physical craft with mouth, arms and legs all involved in the process from standing twiddling the irons in the heat and twirling them like a majorette's baton, to rolling them on a bench and of course the blowing, which magically transforms the fiercely hot molten silica, with its honey-like hue, into a form which becomes quickly recognisable as glass. Time is of the essence. Everything is done free-hand, using calipers for measuring which produces a perfect but hand-made looking result. 'I'm a chaotic, untidy person, but in this studio I am very precise.'

# Larry Skeats
## Retired Shepherd and Publican, Collector of Bygones

Following in his father's and grandfather's footsteps, Larry Skeats was a shepherd for four decades. During that time he worked for Lord Shaftesbury at Wimborne St Giles, the Duke of Wellington and the Crichel Estate.

He moved to Dorset after leaving the army in 1954 and it didn't take long for him to become a much-loved local character, known for selling his shepherd's huts, organising his annual sale of bygones, and charity work. He is also well known locally as ex-Landlord of the Trooper Inn at Stourton Caundle, which he ran for ten years.

Along with his wife, Sue, he puts on 'Call my Bluff' style quizzes where people guess the use of old agricultural tools. He showed us a long pole with metal claws on the end that opened and closed. 'We haven't a clue what it is,' admitted Larry, though suggestions include a snake catcher and a device for pulling out trays from hot ovens. Whatever its purpose, items like it keep his audiences enthralled. To date they have raised well over £15,000 for the Joseph Weld Hospice in Dorchester. Larry also donated all the proceeds from *A Shepherd's Delight*, his book about his life as a Dorset shepherd, to charities for the Blind. 'I've been lucky in life and it's good to give something back,' said Larry from his home near Stalbridge.

# Cliff Standing
## Coursing Greyhound Trainer

With 35 years experience as a professional huntsman and hunt service for nine different packs over that time, it was no wonder that Cliff Standing was feeling 'pretty lost' when he retired in 1988. He got a couple of greyhound puppies so he could pursue his already keen interest in coursing and within a short time he was persuaded to take out a trainers' licence, so he could train dogs for others. At the peak of his career, before the hunting ban of 2005, Cliff Standing had sixteen greyhounds in training. You forget how huge these majestic dogs are, like walking coffee tables with muscles that would make them the envy of any regular gym-goer.

You can tell a dog's potential from approximately two years old. Pace is the essential ingredient. 'They have to be able to turn too, but speed, that's the most important thing,' Cliff told us. Now he has only two dogs in training and goes over to Ireland for about four meetings a year to course. He is grateful to the Irish for allowing an English championship to be set up so those keen on this ancient sport can meet in Ireland, where the sport is still legal.

Completely wild hares are driven by beaters. Once spotted by the slipper (who holds the two competing dogs, one in a red woollen collar, one white) he assesses it to make sure it's a good strong hare then he gives the hare a 100 yard start. He then slips the dogs who chase it until, nearly always, the hare escapes through a hedge and the dogs stop. 'No-one wants to see a hare killed,' said Cliff, clearly upset at the assumption that coursing is cruel, mostly without true knowledge of how it works. 'The hare is free, it goes off and that's it. A few are caught but only the slow or the sick.'

Points are given by the mounted judge to each dog based on its chase and ability to turn, and at the end he waves red or white to show which dog has won. The winner then goes on to the next round in a knock out competition. Apparently the structure of the Wimbledon Lawn Tennis tournament was based on hare coursing, with 64 competitors in a knockout tournament. There's a certain amount of betting, mainly at the bigger meetings. There are approximately fifteen professional trainers nationwide, but anyone can train their own dog and enter the stakes.

Cliff explained all this to us with great patience and care in his deliberate, gravelly voice. Clearly a real countryman with decency and respect for his charges, who were kept in immaculate kennels. They do have one dog who lives in the house but is never run. 'She's difficult to handle, but then she's been spoiled!'

Cliff is proud of having twice won the Swaffham Cup, which was first presented in 1744, 'That meant an awful lot'. He has also won the great Waterloo Cup – the blue riband of the sport. Although Cliff admits the prize money isn't great in coursing, that's not what you do it for.

Cliff offered to show us his dogs in the barn but with a warning. 'I must tell you that they are most unphotogenic. They've always got their ears back and look sulky and horrible.' I'm not sure I agreed with that. They were the most beautiful creatures, and the mutual affection was a great joy.

# Gavin, Matthew and Martin Steeden
## RNLI Volunteers, Swanage Lifeboat Station

Consider for a moment going about your busy daily routine, or sitting relaxing in the evening with friends when a bleeper goes off and you have to drop everything and rush to a lifeboat station, dress in warm and waterproof gear and launch a huge lifeboat to go off in search of a stricken vessel and passengers, probably in bad weather conditions and possibly in the dark. Did I mention you won't get paid for this?

Martin, Gavin and Matt Steeden, father and sons, are three people for whom this is a regular scenario. They are totally committed to helping others and although they admit the whole experience is a 'great buzz', they have to put in a huge amount of time and effort. They train every single Wednesday night, they fund raise and most importantly, they risk their own lives to help others in danger. Martin is Coxswain, as was his father-in-law. Gav and Matt are part of the 25 or so crew, and Martin's young grandsons are already showing a keen interest.

'We spent our childhoods down here with dad being on the crew and on the beach, swimming off the quays. My grandad used to take us out on his boat to go fishing all the time. When I turned 16 he [dad] threw a pager at me and said there you go!' Matt told us.

The commitment needed doesn't suit everyone, but the RNLI always welcomes new recruits, preferably with a little nautical knowledge – though all training is given by the RNLI. 'If you've got a fishing or sailing boat,' said Martin, 'or if you go kayaking and have a basic idea of what the elements will do, that helps. The elements are key to most of what we are doing. Ultimately it's a crew decision as to who joins. If they are good enough they are good enough. It doesn't matter if they are male or female. We have a great time but you never know what you are going to get until you get out to sea.

'We care about what we do and we want to do what we do well. It sounds cheesy but it's the same thing that drives every single lifeboat station. You are proud of what you do and you want to do it to the best of your ability. It is a very unique organisation. We don't seek admiration.'

Martin hesitated before answering my question as to which was the most dramatic rescue in which he had been involved. 'You can say big winds, dark at night, helicopters, boats falling over. They all add to the drama, but there are other things equally testing – everything has its own angle if you like.'

He described being called out to a yacht under full sail. The man had fallen overboard, leaving his wife sailing off into the wide blue yonder and unable to stop. Her husband was pinned to the side of the boat but she was not strong enough to haul him back on board.

Martin explained the sort of things that went through his mind when he was on the way to the rescue. 'It's three or four miles off. You've got twenty minutes to work out what to do. Can we pick him up later? Can the helicopter get to him? Lots of scenarios flying round in the passage to the casualty. When you get there it all changes again because you are presented with something else. In that situation the man overboard is potentially dying because he's an old fella, strapped to the side of a boat going along at five or six knots in the splash line made by the boat, so it has all got to happen reasonably quickly. It's always dramatic when you are putting your crew members into a dangerous situation.'

Martin's contribution has been recognised with a bronze medal, but all these volunteers deserve medals for what they do. The RNLI's income is derived solely from donations, and we'd all do well to remember that next time we're tucked up safely on a stormy night.

' . . . big winds, dark at night, helicopters, boats falling over. They all add to the drama, but there are other things equally testing – everything has its own angle if you like.'

# Jim Stewart
## Chief Executive, Poole Harbour Commissioners

Poole Harbour Commissioners was set up by an Act of Parliament in 1895 to conserve, regulate and improve the port and harbour. These days it also has to take into account the requirements of their 200 or so stakeholders – of which Sunseeker is the largest employer. Jim Stewart took over as Chief Executive in 2012 and describes Poole as 'one of the jewels of the south coast'. He and his team of about 100 'feel privileged to be in charge of it, to pass it on to future generations.'

Jim's job includes running the commercial port, providing facilities for the ferries, cruise ships, bulk cargo ships and some special projects. They have been chosen to host EU Maritime Week in 2017, and have plans to build a new £10 million quay by 2015 which will enable them to accommodate up to 30 large cruise ships annually. In 2013 they supported The Venture Cup Powerboat Race.

Jim further explained there are three types of ports in UK; Privatised ports (eg Southampton and Portland), Municipal ports which are run by the local authorities (eg Portsmouth and Weymouth) and then Trust Ports, such as Poole, Newcastle, Dover and London.

'We don't get any funding from government but we generate money from the commercial port and charge harbour dues as well. Effectively any profits that we make we invest back into the business. We pay rates, corporation tax and VAT like any other business. Poole is the fifth biggest of 120 trust ports in the UK in terms of turnover.'

Poole Harbour is the second largest natural harbour in the world, after Sydney. As well as attracting commercial interests, including fishing, a sunny weekend in the summer brings out the passenger boats that ply the Harbour, kayaks, jet skiers, kite and wind surfers, speedboats, and sailing boats of every size and class, from tiny dinghys to 30 metre yachts.

Jim thinks the beauty of Poole Harbour owes a lot to its diversity. It is home to a wonderful array of wildlife, including the largest population of seahorses in the UK. Jim mentioned that you often see deer swimming between the Harbour's five islands, or from the mainland. There is a constant stream of marine biologists surveying the area and there are protected sites of special scientific interest and marine conservation zones.

As well as his various responsibilities running the port and Harbour, Jim holds national positions, including Chairman of Maritime UK, and Chairman of British Ports Association. He originally moved to Southampton, having worked in London and Kent, came to look at Poole and loved it. 'You get sucked into Dorset and you never want to leave; I think that's where I am at the moment actually.'

We were fortunate enough to meet the Harbour Master, Brian Murphy, on the day of our visit, who kindly gave us a boat tour of the Harbour. We ended up by one of the huge buoys which mark the main channels for incoming ferries and cargo boats. This particular buoy was called Diver, but no-one can remember why. The same applies to Aunt Betty, Jack Jones, Punch and Judy – adding just a small measure of mystery to a Harbour whose long past faces a fascinating future.

# Michael Stoate
## Miller

The Stoate family have been millers in the West Country for generations and, although Michael doesn't remember being coerced into joining the family business, he thinks he may have been cleverly steered by his father. Michael was interested in engineering, and fixing the seemingly innumerable number of machines needed to work a mill did, and still does, give him great pleasure.

The traditional mill at Cann near Shaftesbury, where Michael was born and grew up, has a huge water wheel, which dates back to the 1880s, situated in the centre of the fairly modern building. It is the only commercial water-powered mill left in the county. The mill itself is a Dorset landmark, thanks to the Portugese style windmill built on the roof in 1971.

The original mill building burned down in the 1950s which Michael regards as a blessing, as not being listed has enabled him to modernise where necessary. They still use a special French burr stone for grinding the grain, as the hard limestone is slightly porous and abrasive which is good for separating the bran from the flour. Traditionally Derbyshire peak stone was used in British milling but French burr is preferable for the tougher bread-making flour. It is quite a sight, and sound, to witness the water gushing round the overshot wheel and the various belts turning cogs all around the mill floor. Though it is obviously a highly efficient set up, one can't help but feel there is something wonderfully Heath Robinson about the arrangement.

Stoates largely supply their range of twelve flours, which include the award-winning Organic Maltstar and Organic Stoneground Strong White, to independent bakers and health food shops. Michael isn't interested in supplying to supermarkets. Of the 500 or so tonnes of flour they produce each year a proportion is delivered to their customers on a regular basis: on the day of our visit Michael was preparing for the Cornwall run, which meant a 4 a.m. start the next day.

They use local grain when possible, but it is obviously dependent upon availability. Michael is not expecting the Somerset Levels to produce any wheat this year because of the winter flooding. He has been using grain from Tarrant Launceston, and also imports from Canada, Ukraine and Kazakhstan, whose grain is particularly well suited for bread-making flour.

Even at nine in the morning Michael Stoate was covered in a light dusting of flour, though because of the dangers of breathing too much flour in, he and his staff wear protective helmets when milling to guard against farmer's lung.

There is almost no wastage, with any chaff or grain from the grain feeder going for fodder. They can be troubled by the flour moth, which are monitored constantly. Rats are kept well under control, though in Michael's father's day they did have a complaint from a customer who, whilst helping themselves to Stoates flour in a wholefood shop, found a set of rat's teeth in their scoop (happily it was finally established that the teeth came from an open sack of rice nearby).

It is evidently not an easy life being a miller, even with the benefit of modern machinery. Michael seems to thrive on it though. 'I haven't finished yet,' he told me. 'Always learning. That's the fun of it, blending new and old technologies together, that's the challenge. I am not going to mess with the traditional ways of milling flour but it's good to find ways to make it easier.'

# John Stockley
## Chimney Sweep

'You can't be more Dorset than me – apart from the African American bit!'

John 'Sooty' Stockley has had a colourful life. He never knew his father, who was an African American GI, so was brought up by his mother and stepfather – who was also a chimney sweep. Now retired, his son James has taken over the business, although John does turn up at weddings in traditional sweep's costume to wish people good luck on their wedding day. He also occasionally gives after dinner speeches.

He was born and brought up in Fleet, where his grandfather was the village sweep. He then moved to Weymouth but has lived and worked all over the world. 'I love my town, I love Dorset. I'm an Englishman first and foremost. When I was 23, in the 1960s, I had a pub in Weymouth called the Globe and was the first black landlord on the south coast I think, certainly the youngest. Graffiti in the pub used to say Britannia Rules the World but Sooty rules the Globe!'

John's mother was from Burton Bradstock, 'You can't be more Dorset than me – apart from the African American bit!'

He loves joking about his colourful ancestry, saying he's an Anglo Afro American and is called Sooty because of the job, not because of his colour. John told us that as a chimney sweep you get to know your clients. 'Ninety per cent of the time you're dealing with the lady of the house. So in a way you become like a social worker. You'd be surprised what people confide, even though you only see them once a year. But because you are in their house to do its dirtiest job they trust you.'

Apart from the gossip another perk is that anything in the chimney belongs to the sweep – as long as it comes down. 'I was doing a big house, sweeping a bedroom chimney with a massive nest in it as it hadn't been used for 150 years. I was finishing it off when I heard this metallic sound in the chimney and a Georgian silver serving spoon fell down in front of me. Jackdaws would have taken it. Legally the spoon is mine, so I kept it. That law goes back to Henry VIII.'

# Dave Symonds
## Thatcher

Dave has been thatching for fifty years and doesn't seem to be slowing up, especially now his son has joined the business. 'Things aren't how they used to be,' he told us. 'Different class of people living down here now and that's changing it slightly.' But despite the changes, Dave and his son and their three other employees thatched around 150 roofs last year, so he is never idle, despite his body feeling a bit creaky some mornings.

Dave estimates there are over 600 thatchers nationwide, 30 or 40 of them in Dorset. Dave himself also farms 60 acres where he grows his own wheat straw which is combed to produce the good straight, long stems used for thatching. The grain is sold for animal feed and the remainder baled up for animal bedding. Occasionally they use reed imported from Turkey but this is rare. A pity, some would argue, as it lasts up to forty years, much more than the traditional local variety.

Jackdaws, rats and smaller birds can be a nuisance, but not bats. Dave loves bats and they live inside the roof so don't bother him. 'We never bump into each

'In the old days we'd have had swallows buzzing up and down the main street all the summer long.'

other hardly at all, and they don't harm anybody, do they? Jackdaws nick the long lengths of straw and keep dropping them down the closest chimney until they lodge across because it saves going off to get twigs. Rats are an age old problem. They'll do a lot of damage to a roof if they choose to climb up a bush or something and get in.'

He's sad about the lack of places for swallows to nest in. Outbuildings and houses are done up to such a high standard they can't find nesting sites under the eaves. 'In the old days we'd have had swallows buzzing up and down the main street all the summer long.'

Dave proudly told us he is becoming a bit of a You Tube hit with a film showing him muffling the bells at St Giles Church, Chideock, where he is Captain of the Bells. Dave loves the slower pace of life in Dorset and its way of doing things. He's lived in the Chideock area all his life and has 'never wanted to live anywhere else'. With his vertiginous life style, be it roof or bell tower, I expect he sees more of Dorset than most of us.

# Cyril Tite
## Scrap Metal Merchant and Collector

Cyril was asleep when we arrived. He was settled in his chair at the kitchen table, mouth slightly open, snoozing in a warm corner of his empire. A shock of silver white hair shone out amongst the gloom, and its dusty piles of bottles, ornaments, papers, clocks, books, trays, pictures, lights and bric-a-brac.

He moved to Lyons Gate from Alton Pancras as a four-year old in 1926 with his parents, by horse and cart. He now lives on his own in his bungalow and his sons, Geoff and John, run the car breaking yard and garage, leaving him time for his collecting.

'I expect I'll do damage to the camera,' Cyril joked, when finally awake. 'Crikey. I always wear a tie. I done everything. Cattle lorries, hauling, all sorts.'

We tactfully enquired about the remarkable amount of stuff crammed into Cyril's home and adjacent sheds. 'Loads of it I got. I buy all over the place. Someone came from Holland the other day and bought a few things. People know about me. I've people coming from all over the country and Canada, America. Just bought some drainpipes from France. Collected all my life I suppose. I got loads in here and loads in there and loads in another room, loads of it. I got bottles, all sizes, everything. All sorts of crockery and loads and loads of books. I clear out places for people.'

'Of all the things you've collected what do you like the best?'

'Money!'

'Where would you go if you could go anywhere?'

'Nowhere. Don't want to go anywhere.'

'Just Dorset?'

'Yeah, just Dorset . . . just Lyons Gate.'

# Charlie Waite
## Landscape Photographer

As we chatted at his peaceful, riverside home, Charlie Waite marvelled at the beauty of his surroundings. His enthusiasm and real passion for life are infectious and it was a joy to be with someone so alive.

Charlie began as an actor who in turn went on to take portrait photographs of his fellow actors

or effort is always accompanied by monumental insecurity.'

Charlie tries to convey what landscape photography can do for your soul, to show how the camera and photograph express and reflect back a response to the world around you. He thinks the landscape photographer needs to own the view in its entirety. 'Sometimes it's really elusive but you can't let it go.'

'I want to stand where Ansel Adams stood. I'm a groupie. He is my mentor, partly because he was a great artist and great technician rolled into one, and he had wonderful lines like "recognition and previsualisation blended together in a single moment of awareness". That really is him, head turning in slow motion, seeing, responding and recognising, and then its a question of tripod, camera, what I call feet of clay, getting it all set up and then trying to find parity between the perfect and what is actually out there. The nearer the two can be together, the less compromises to make.

'I think it's almost a curse to be a landscape photographer, partly because you can't stop responding. You can't stop recognising and then you can't really let it go, that's the thing. I can't believe it's any different to the composer, to the cook, to the person who can only really express what they want to express by writing, by painting, by sculpting. I don't think you can switch off. It is so sad when you see people who haven't got the time to be creative.'

We asked Charlie for his favourite view in Dorset. We got a wonderfully descriptive reply. 'For all I know it might be here – this garden. I'm sure there are better views, whatever a better view is, but I get such huge pleasure from the aesthetics of this little scene. It is just ridiculous, almost divine, an image of your imagination. The boat just sits there; my wife brilliantly painted it red and it's named after a dog we had, called Alfie. When the sun goes down you cannot look at that bit of water at the end of the island it is so bright, so shiny and then an egret suddenly arrives and it's just pulsating all around it. It's an amazing mobile scene and now I don't know what I'd do if I had to look at something that didn't move.'

before a chance meeting led him into landscape photography. Today he is internationally known: a presenter of television programmes, author of books of landscape photography, and founder of 'Light and Land', a company organising photographic tours. Despite such fame,  in his charming, self-deprecating way Charlie still believes that 'any artistic endeavour

# Harry Warr
## Gamekeeper and River Keeper

Although there was no hiding Harry's huge smile and big laugh, his friend, Joe Allen, a keeper from Portland, told us that Harry was a bit shy with us. 'On a shoot,' Joe told us, 'Harry doesn't need a radio. His voice carries! People know him all over the country and from all walks of life.'

Harry himself tells us he meets all sorts out shooting, some a little more appealing than others.'It's certainly very concerning to me that a lot of the people coming shooting today never came in as young children trained by their fathers. They now start when they've got that level of affluence, and financial backing to be able to do it. It's an expensive hobby, game shooting. They think it's the right thing to do and that's the wrong way. I've had a lot of dealings with the likes of Joe and me and people at the top. I quite like them. The ones in the middle step on you, trying to get up the ladder a bit further.'

Harry's life as a river keeper keeps him busy but hasn't made him rich. 'You need the right woman as a

wife to put up with it. Suits some women, doesn't suit a lot. There's hell of a lot of divorces in keepers.'

Harry was born in Dorset and all his family is here. When we met he was on his fifth season on the East Burton Estate. He worked on the Wrackleford Estate for four years and has been a head keeper in Dorset, Devon, Shropshire, Kent and North Wales.

These days he is semi-retired, but loves the life of the river. His days are spent improving the fishes' habitat by removing weeds whilst still preserving a natural refuge for the trout and the insect life on which they feed. He has to make sure the water is free from pollution, maintain its banks, and manage predators such as mink, cormorants and herons.

His dog Jet – 'a working cock up!'– goes everywhere with him. Harry is a softie with him and you can tell why. 'I spoil him I do. I got another in the kennel, brown one. This one don't work; I'd spend half the day lookin' for 'im. My Mrs reckons we'd be divorced over it. Jet get off me trousers!'

Lieutenant General Sir Barney White-Spunner has played key roles in world conflicts of recent times and, having met him, I have no doubt that any decisions he made were for the good. He lacks pomposity and arrogance and talks about his career in a very matter of fact way – saying it 'was hugely interesting at the time' and, of his time at the top, 'I was the Army Commander but I wasn't the one who sits in London. I did the everyday running of the thing from Andover, which was fun and a nice job to finish up with.' Though retired, he retains a military link as Colonel of the Royal Yeomanry.

Sir Barney's career started in 1979 when he was commissioned into the Blues and Royals. He became Commanding Officer of the Household Cavalry, was deployed to Bosnia and on promotion to Colonel became Deputy Director of Defence Policy at NATO. In 2002 he was given command of the Kabul Multinational Brigade and then became Chief of Joint Force Operations for the national contingent in the Middle East. In 2005 he became Chief of Staff at Land Command and two years later was appointed General Officer Commanding 3rd (UK) Mechanised Division with whom he was deployed to Iraq. He went on to become Commander of the Field Army in 2009.

So long and distinguished a career is bound to have its share of stories, but Sir Barney was particularly fascinating about his involvement in disarming the Albanian Liberation Army in Macedonia in 2001, shortly before 9/11. After that, in December 2001, he went to Kabul to try and take out the Al Quaeda training bases and the Taliban.

It was a far cry from his first visit to Afghanistan, where as a student many years earlier he had hitch-hiked round the south of the country. 'I raided everybody's address books before I went and discovered my sister had a friend who was working in the British Embassy in Kabul. We banged on the gates of the compound and a very polite Gurkha let in two, very scruffy student backpackers, who were filthy and probably stinking to high heaven!' They were given a cup of tea in smart Embassy china by the swimming pool and had a lovely time.

'Fast forward to coming back in 2001. The British

Embassy had been ransacked and burned to the ground and there was just one little cottage left in the corner.' As they moved into the city to clear the Taliban out, Barney went in there to see what could be salvaged of the Embassy. Amazingly, there was the same Gurkha who had given them sustenance all those years ago, with the same china, bringing out a cup of tea. He had kept that bit of the embassy safe and guarded the Union Jack.

Since 2012, Barney has been Executive Chairman of the Countryside Alliance. His love of the countryside is obvious and he really cares about the issues he is trying to resolve. People mistakenly think of the CA as a hunting pressure group but it is so much more than that, with affordable rural housing, mobile phone signals and wider broadband coverage as top priorities.

We talked about the recent controversial badger cull and,, as Barney explained 'We all love badgers, but that doesn't mean you don't need to control them. We

# Lieutenant General Sir Barney White-Spunner KCB, CBE
## Chairman, The Countryside Alliance

all want a healthy badger population; the last thing you want is poor old diseased badgers. Have you ever seen a badger with TB? It's a nasty sight. One of the principles we stand for is having balanced and responsible management of the countryside. So we don't approve of having a specific Act of Parliament to protect one species, like a badger, when you don't, for example, have one to protect the hedgehog, which the badgers have almost wiped out. You have got to have a balance.'

In his work with Catholic Aid for Overseas Development (he is Chairman of the Development board), he has travelled to Africa and is struck by the difference in attitude between the population of a country like Zambia, where food production is everything and people have got to be fed, and here where food production is not really considered anymore and is taken for granted.

After talking to us Barney took us up to his favourite view from Pilsdon Penn overlooking the Marshwood Vale. He was brought up with the Blackmore Vale on his doorstep and later moved to Winsham and has ended up near Pilsdon, which he considers 'one of the most unspoilt bits of England left.'

# Peter Wilson
## Shooter, Olympic Gold Medallist

I wish I could share the secret to Peter Wilson's Olympic success. His training programme, overseen by Sheikh Ahmed of Dubai, is secret. Super secret. Peter tells us that every one of those in the 2012 Olympic double trap competition had the technical proficiency to win but, when it came down to it, the inner strength, mental energy, edge, whatever you call it, that Peter had acquired from the many years preparation prior to 2012, is what made the difference.

Peter talked me through that life-changing day. 'I walked round to start the last five pairs. I shot peg one and as I walked on I remember looking at the board and thinking, my god, four targets clear of second place and thought, this is it I've won the Olympics. There's no way in hell I'm going to miss four targets now to draw. I was buzzing. Wasn't even focussed on what I was doing then and went miss, miss, and my

mouth just dropped.

'I realised all of a sudden that it was going to be a lot harder than I had anticipated. It is very easy to miss two in the last four. Suddenly the pressure is right on you and I went pair kill, pair kill, pair kill and I had to get one out of the last two, and I hit both of them. I think I aged about ten years in that moment!

'So much has happened since and you suddenly realise what is out there for you, when you win Gold at the Olympics. It is a different world. I know more than ever now that it is not what you know, but who you know. I've met some incredibly rich and influential people who make things happen. You say, I'd like to do this, and they reply, "let's do it!"'

Peter's philosophy is 'be the best I can be and if that meant I won an Olympic event, so be it.' He explained that he didn't want to be one of those old men whose grandchildren say, 'My granddad could have gone to the Olympics.' He would rather his grandchildren said, 'He did his best and it wasn't good enough, or he did his best and won a medal at the Olympics.'

He wonders if his determination comes from being picked on as a child. 'I was always the tallest at school and it was really infuriating because if anything went wrong or anyone got punched, and I was there, it was my fault and I was always being dragged into the headmaster. I think that makes you much more resilient; you just have to get on with life.'

In Peter's opinion, sportsmen and women fall into two brackets. You either love winning or hate losing; Peter hates losing. He tries not to put too much emphasis on the gun. Guns often go missing in transit. Right now his gun is exactly as he wants it, he only has one, but with spare parts. It is so finely tuned that it would take him six months to get another one to the same state of perfection. He will be beginning his preparation for the next Olympics soon, though he is also coaching a young teenager from Yorkshire showing exceptional promise.

Before his extraordinary Olympic success Peter struggled to earn his living but now he gets flights, hotels, training and a good income from UK Sport. He is sponsored by the gunmakers Holland and Holland, and Gleneagles. He has found the right balance between competing and his commercial commitments, whilst still allowing time for his business interests, in developing shooting apps for tablets such as the iPad.

Peter, an only child who is Dorset born and bred, loves his county. He is travelling half the year now so appreciates coming home even more. When I asked him how he would like to describe his occupation for the book his first reply was 'farmer'. I think that says it all!

# The Yetties
## Folk Band

Back in the 1960's, four young local boys, John 'Bonny' Sartin, Mac McCulloch, Pete Shutler and Bob Common met at the Yetminster Scouts. The local WI started folk dancing lessons and the four teenagers soon discovered that you could cuddle the girls at a dancing lesson without getting your hand slapped!

Ever enthusiastic, the newly formed Yetminster and Ryme Intrinseca Junior Folk Dance Display Team were on a bus en route to a folk festival when the driver, having difficulty with the lengthy name of the group, called out for 'The Yetties' to disembark. The name stuck and 50 years later, though officially retired, they still perform together on occasions as a trio; Bob left the group in 1979.

The Yetties began their professional career in 1967. Bonny was the lead singer, Pete played keyboard, accordion, penny whistle, concertina and bowed psaltery (similar to a zither) and Mac, guitar and banjo. They travelled all over the world, sent there by the British Council to spread British culture, particularly in the Far East. They worked for the BBC on programmes such as 'Friday Night is Music Night' and their regular Radio 2 series, 'Cider & Song', bringing brightness and cheer to a huge following at

home and abroad.

Audience participation has always been a really important part of their act and key to their success. From the very beginning they tried to produce entertainment for all the family with a humorous element. Under different labels, The Yetties recorded 45 albums, their debut album released in 1969 was 'Fifty Stone of Loveliness'. They have played songs using Thomas Hardy's own fiddle, and a joint project with John Arlott recording music about cricketers of the past. They sang traditional Dorset numbers as well as new ones by a variety of writers, including Bonny. Audiences most frequently requested 'Fiddlers Green', though 'Dorset is Beautiful' achieved the highest rating in the charts.

The lyrics recalled childhood memories of helping farmers at harvest time, scrumping for apples, and raiding the hedges, fields and woods for food. Their

music brings to life the atmosphere of rural life and its characters. 'With our singing,' said Pete, 'we were talking about things we knew about in a genuine Dorset accent so it came over that we were real – the genuine article. We were the country bumpkins.

'Late night travelling was hard work but there is no doubt for three country lads to go out and do the things we did, we were lucky dogs!'

They've had some fun over the years and wouldn't change a thing. On some occasions they didn't know whether to 'play faster or stop playing.' One lady, evidently moved by the music, started taking her clothes off. They decided it was better to keep playing; keeping the audience happy always being their priority!

Despite international success and a huge following they have never forgotten their roots, all agreeing that 'Dorset is a lovely place to come home to.'

# List of Subscribers

The publisher would like to thank all those whose names are listed below,
as well as the subscribers who chose to remain anonymous.
Their support helped make this book possible.

Sir Antony and Lady Acland
Papi Aguirrezabal
William and Sally Alden
K. Amin
Jane and Mark Anderson
Rebecca and Hugo Andreae
Giorgia Arnold
Emma Atkinson-Willes
Matt and Alix Austen

Tim and Natasha Bailey
Desmond Baker
Tim and Annie Balkwill
Nigel A. Ball
R.A. Bambrough
The Barandiaran Muguruza Family
Laura and David Barbour
Justin and Harriet Baring
Janet V. Bassett
Beverley Bassinger
Simon and Victoria Baxter
David and Sally Beaton
Graham and Margaret Birch
Joyce Bishop (Minc)
Kathy Booth
Peter Bowring
Ali and Tim Boylan
Jez Bragg
Frank and Caro Brand
Victoria Bridgeman-Sutton
Pippa Brierley
Lucy Bromhead
Charles and Beatrice Brown
Iain Burnett

Sally Cairns
Charles Du Cane
Annabel and Mark Carr
The Carter Family
Penelope Cherry
Biddy Chittenden
Justin Chittenden and family
Oliver and Emily Chittenden
Rosanna Chittenden
Charlie and Mindy Clarke
Scarlett and India Cole
Mr John A. Cook
Angelica and Eddie Cotterell
Richie and Jill Courtauld
Mike and Sarah Covell
Henrietta and Rob Crittall

Patricia Daniels
Antonia and Mark Davies
Michael Davies
Tom and Emma Davies
Mr and Mrs A. Davis
Richard and Lisa Dennis
Andrew Thomas Dike
Luci and Charles Downing
Martin R.A. Duffy

Clare Ellwood

Bridget Fairlie
Mark and Lizzie Fenwick
Caroline Fiennes
Chris Finch
Willa Franks

Campbell and Miranda Fraser
Graham and Norah French
Stephen Fudge

Anthony and Annie Garnett
Adrian and Janie Garnon
Jamie Giles
The Hon Mrs C. Girkins
Claire and James Godman-
    Dorington
Norman and Henrietta Gold
Bertie and Sarah Gore-Browne
Ann Grafton
Susan Grahame
P. Green Esq.
Henry Groves

Christine Hatch
Joy I. Hawkins
Gillian and Ivan Hayward
Hazelbury Bryan Primary School
Pete and Becca Heath
The Hewlett Family
Peter Hills
Rory and Sophie Hills and family
Giulietta and Peter Horner
The Hosford Family
Hotel Rural Casa de la Veiga
Donna Howard

Ted Ingram

Amanda Jackson-Sytner
Nick and Zara Jeffery

The Johnsen Family
Beatrice Niamh Junor

Charlotte Kennedy
Charlie and Talita Kimmins
The Kimmins Family

Monica Laiseca Hoffmeyer
Angela Langford
Max and Oli Laughland
Dione Lawrence
Richard Le Fleming
Caroline Leng
M.P. Lewis
Justin and Margo Liddle

Angus and Katherine Macdonald
James and Vanessa Macdonald
Catherine Macmillan
Mark and Gemma Malley
Tory Manuel
Lord Margadale
Jenny Marsh
Alice Martin & Alfie Millar
Gigi and Cathal McCosker
Tilly McMaster and Simon Akroyd
Joan McNabb
Emma and James McVittie
Charlie and Ruth Middle
Lucinda Miller
Katie Quentin Mills
Sheila Montague
Amanda Moorhouse

David J. Morris
Iris Morris
Ian and Pip Morison
Joanne Myram, Positive PR

Rupert and Theresa Newell

John Philip O'Dwyer
Judy Ogilvie

The Pérez De Saralegui Family
Ed and Catharine Pyke
Christopher and Gina Pilkington
Ian and Penny Pilkington
Nick and Gabriela Pilkington
J.W.W. Pittard
George and Camilla Ponsonby
Frank Pope
Oliver and Katie Pope
The Present Finder
Judith and Tim Price

Candice Raby
Lucia Real de Asua
Michael and Victoria Regan
Catherine and Simon Rennie
Alexa and Mark Ridley
C. and A. Risby
Guillermo Rivera
Rupert and Georgina Robson
Richard Roberts
Tom Rushton
Ryder and Sarah Ryan

Kate and Iain Saker
John Shorto
Larry Skeats
Sheila Roberta Smith
Tom and Holly Spenlove-Brown
Phyllida Stanley
Melissa Stourton

Matt and Catty Thomas
Clive Thorp
Richard and Sue Timmis
Paul N. Tory

Mark Valder
Alex and Clare Van Moppes
The Varley Family
Zara and Ali Vaux

Charlie Waite
C. Went
Mr and Mrs Westlake
Claire and Hugh Whitworth
Madeleine Wickham
Nigel and Karen Williams
Otto Williams
Maria and Edward Wingfield Digby
Stephen and Sylvia Wingfield Digby
Roger and Penny Wort
Roderick Wurfbain

Anthony Yeatman
Jane and Simon Yorke